Staying Focused

In A Hyper World:

Book One

BOOKS BY JOHN GRAY, PH.D.

Men are from Mars Women are from Venus (HarperCollins, 1992)

What You Feel, You Can Heal (Heart Publishing, 1984)

Men, Women and Relationships (Beyond Words Publishing, 1993)

Mars and Venus in the Bedroom (HarperCollins, 1995)

Mars and Venus Together Forever (Harper Perennial, 1996)

Mars and Venus in Love (HarperCollins, 1996)

Mars and Venus on a Date (Harper Collins, 1997)

Mars and Venus Starting Over (HarperCollins, 1998)

Men Are from Mars, Women Are from Venus Book of Days (HarperCollins, 1998)

How *to Get What You Want and Want What You Have* (HarperCollins, 1999)

Children Are from Heaven (HarperCollins, 1999)

Practical Miracles for Mars and Venus (HarperCollins, 2000)

How to Get What You Want at Work (HarperCollins 2002)

Truly Mars and Venus (HarperCollins, 2003)

The Mars and Venus Diet and Exercise Solution (St. Martin's Press, 2003)

Why Mars and Venus Collide (HarperCollins, 2008)

Venus on Fire Mars on Ice (Mind Publishing, 2010)

Work With Me (Palgrave Macmillan, 2013)

Staying Focused In A Hyper World: Book One

NATURAL SOLUTIONS FOR ADHD, MEMORY AND BRAIN PERFORMANCE

JOHN GRAY, PH.D.

Staying Focused in A Hyper World: Book 1; Natural Solutions for
ADHD, Memory and Brain Performance

ISBN: 978-0-9903468-0-7

www.MarsVenus.com

*I dedicate this book to
my daughter, Lauren,
whose commitment to
relationships, health and happiness
inspired me to develop
the many ideas in this book.*

Contents

Acknowledgements

I want to thank my wife, Bonnie Gray, for thirty years of her devoted love and support. I also want to thank our three daughters and their partners, Shannon and Jon, Juliet and Dan, Lauren and Glade, and to our adorable grandchildren Sophia, Bo, Brady, and Makena. Without Bonnie's support I could not have written this book and sustained a successful career, a loving family and great health.

So many thanks go to my team that makes this work happen. I want to thank Hallina Popko my executive assistant, Jon Myers my marketing director for MarsVenus.com, Marcy Wynne, director of customer service, Glade Truitt director of video production for my online blogs and Web design, Jeff Owens director of AskMarsVenus.com, and all of the Mars Venus Life Coaches around the world. Special thanks to my daughter Lauren Gray for her popular Video Blogs at MarsVenus.com.

I want to thank the team at Amazon.com for their continued support in publishing this book and Teri Smart and Blake Lefkoe for doing the final proofreading.

A big thanks goes to the many researchers in health and wellness who have made this book possible and the parents who have trusted these ideas to not only improve their marriages but have given their children the opportunity to restore normal brain function and begin developing and expressing their full potential for happiness, learning and success.

Foreword

For many people today, we live in a time of unprecedented wealth and comfort: you and me and many of our friends. From a historical perspective we've never had it so good. Just a few generations ago, our ancestors suffered from terrible circumstances which today we have eliminated from our lives: rickets, scurvy, polio and hundreds more maladies were still commonplace at the end of the 19th century. Millions of people died of the flu in 1919, a condition which today is rarely fatal. Childbirth until recently was also a potentially fatal experience, for both mother and baby. If you had the misfortune to suffer from a mental illness, like anxiety, depression, or a more serious condition like schizophrenia, you could have been subjected to painful electric shock treatments and confinement for life in an asylum. Many of the terrible afflictions that plagued humanity are gone. From this perspective we live in a paradise hardly dreamed possible by our great grandparents.

We live in a paradise hardly dreamed possible by our great grandparents.

Despite so much progress in medicine and technology, we still suffer, don't we? The family unit, the crowning achievement of a civilized society is breaking apart. Every year more people are getting divorced and even more are choosing to not even get married. Children and teenagers today in particular suffer,

and perhaps the greatest source of that suffering, even for afflu-
ent people in the Western world today, is the increasing trend of
various mental challenges often bundled together in the name of
ADHD.

If you have ever suffered from an inability to focus, whether
in a full-blown form with the diagnosis of ADHD or in a
milder version, which afflicts so many more people, you probably know the depth of frustration, anxiety and regret which
so often accompanies this condition. Ironically it is a condition
affecting some of the most creative, brilliant and innovative
minds in today's world. As a result, millions of children, teens
and adults are overwhelmed, distracted and sometimes immo-
bilized by the ever- increasing stimulation and stress from our
busy lives.

Ironically, ADHD is a condition
affecting some of the most creative,
brilliant and innovative minds in today's world.

Maybe you know what it's like when you have a deadline to
keep and you have every good intention of not disappointing people. You sit down at your computer or workplace to "get on with
it." And then it starts. Facebook, email, checking on the laundry,
getting a snack, the latest update on CNN, texts, tweets, you find
yourself lost in a seemingly unavoidable string of distractions, until
you finally slink off to bed in defeat at the end of the day, with
almost no real progress made.

One of the great difficulties with the inability to control or
direct your attention is that it is not widely recognized as an
affliction at all. People might call you "flaky" or "irresponsible,"
or simply think you don't care about them. Ironically the more
behind you get, the more stressed you feel, and that stress itself
makes it harder and harder to stay focused.

With ADHD, people might call you
"flaky" or "irresponsible,"
or simply think you don't care about them.

Not only the people close to you cease to trust you, it is even more devastating than that. You cease to trust yourself. If you suffer from the inability to hold attention, you could sit down to do your taxes, or to file a report, or to work on your great contribution to the world, already knowing full well at the start the day that you will not get very far. The inability to purposely focus your attention can be the most reliable way to erode self-esteem, and to give up on yourself and your dreams.

I can tell you about these things with some degree of familiarity, and compassion, because I suffered from attention deficit disorder, albeit in its milder and more manageable version, most of my life. I know full well what it's like to let people down on deadlines, despite my best intentions. I know what its like to start off with enthusiasm to get things done, and to collapse in defeat a few hours later. As this book points out, because ADHD is so determined by brain chemistry, which is in turn highly influenced by both genetics and environmental conditions, it is often passed on from one generation to the other.

ADHD parents are likely to have ADHD children. And so it was painful to watch my younger son sit down time after time with his teachers, and make fresh promises about getting caught up with his schoolwork, and then fail to keep his word. I watched helplessly, almost like seeing an accident happen in slow motion, as his grades went down semester after semester. Homework was late or got lost, despite my best intentions to be the homework police. I saw him slowly give up, not only on schoolwork, but also on himself and his own future. He got used to being thought of as a flaky guy.

"I watched helplessly, almost like seeing
an accident happen in slow motion,
as his grades went down semester after semester."

I was very lucky at that period in my life to be in a men's group with John Gray, who I have known for 35 years. He told me about some of the most simple remedies, natural substances from plants and real food, that are highly effective alternatives to pharmaceutical drugs like Ritalin, and that have no negative side effects. I started to use his mineral orotates, his shake with un-denatured whey protein, and vitamin C taken together with grape seed extract. I followed his advice to eat eggs for breakfast. I made changes in diet, and exercised more regularly. All of this was delightfully inexpensive, and easy to integrate into my life. I noticed dramatic and immediate changes in the way my own brain was functioning. As a result, I was able to finish a book in three months, where previously it had taken me years. Since making simple adjustments to my diet and lifestyle, I've been able to serve so many more people, and give my gift more easily.

But even more important, and an even greater relief to me, was that my son also adopted some of the same changes. He was able to graduate high school with honor, and is now doing what he really loves. At 18 he is a ski coach at one of America's most prestigious ski resorts, and he has coached kids to compete in national championships. He is living his dream life and making good money doing what he loves, which at 18 is nothing short of a miracle.

My son came very close to a dangerously steep and slippery downhill slope of being diagnosed as having a "condition," then needing medication prescribed by an expert, and then potentially spiraling out of control as a permanent misfit and failure. This happened to several of his peers at school. It happens to millions of kids every year.

The diagnosis of ADHD and the inability of allopathic medicine to do anything about it is our modern tragedy. It is the 21st century's version of rickets, polio, or scurvy. My son narrowly escaped that fate, not by being cured by the system, but through our good fortune of having a friend who questions the very foundation on which the modern medical system is built.

The use of drugs to treat ADHD is our modern tragedy.

This is a brilliant book by a very brilliant man who has the compassion, the intelligence, and the courage to take on a predicament that is possibly one of the greatest sources of suffering in our culture: our inability to stay focused on what is most important while living in our new fast paced and hyper world.

Arjuna Ardagh

Founder of Awakening Coaching and author of *Better than Sex* and seven other books.

Second Foreword

There are so few times in life when we get a do-over and if you get one it is few and far between. If you are lucky enough to get a do-over, I suggest you take it.

There are also few rare times when you meet a person by chance—someone who profoundly changes your life and the lives of your children forever. I find myself as one of the lucky ones who got a do-over, and who was lucky enough to meet a visionary, by chance, whose willingness to share his knowledge changed my life and the life of my son forever.

In 2003, my life changed on a beautiful August afternoon when I met Dr. John Gray. John was at a book signing of his newly released book, *The Mars Venus Diet and Exercise Solution*. As the world-famous author was signing my book he just happened to ask about my family. I shared that I have two wonderful sons, Drew the oldest and Colin, the youngest.

I told John about Drew, a graduate of the University of Colorado in Boulder. I then told him about Colin. Colin, I shared, was a gifted athlete who seemed to have everything going for him. I further revealed the terrible struggles that Colin was having, suffering from an inability to concentrate along with extreme anxiety and depression—something I came to find that many young people suffer from today.

"John," I said. "It's heartbreaking to see Colin struggle so with his life. It's even more heart breaking to think that I can't do more to comfort Colin."

John Gray who I had just met showed a sincere and genuine interest in Colin. He said to me the words that will forever ring in my head as a parent,

"Peter, what does your son eat?"

I proceeded to tell him what Colin ate which consisted of high sugary soft drinks, almost no vegetables and lots of burgers and fries.

I will never forget the smile that came over John's face as he then said, "Peter I have discovered new all natural nutritional protocols that have had some amazing results with kids with ADD, ADHD, Depression and Anxiety. If you will follow what I tell you to do then we can really help Colin."

**New nutritional protocols can have amazing results
for kids with ADD, ADHD, depression and anxiety.**

The first thing that entered my mind was we already had Colin on prescription drugs. I didn't think he should take any more. After only a few weeks, Colin stopped taking them saying that he did not feel "real." He felt as if he was living behind a glass wall.

He said, "Dad, even though the drugs helped me to concentrate, they make me feel unreal. They make me feel like someone I do not know."

After talking with John, I would be lying if I did not say I was very skeptical. After all, what could natural solutions do when even drugs had failed to help Colin.

John had such confidence and conviction that I thought, "Ok, what do I have to lose? As I returned home I knew that I was willing to try what he had shared. As it turned out Colin was very resistant and we literally had to force him to try it. He said it was a stupid idea, that it would not work as nothing else had worked.

Fortunately, Colin somehow managed to overcome his great resistance and went on the protocol.

Colin began on a Monday morning but by Tuesday he again stated that it was not going to work. I pleaded with him to just give it a few more days. That Friday morning, five short days later, Colin came to me with a look on his face that I had not seen before and stated, "Dad I don't know what the heck is in this stuff but I feel better than I have felt since I was a little kid."

We hugged one another for the longest time and, with tears streaming down our faces, Colin said, "Dad I think my life has changed and I feel like I have hope for my future."

That was nearly 11 years ago. Colin continues to thrive most of the time. He has his moments but that is generally when he has strayed from the protocol John recommended, but fortunately Colin finds that he is always able to course correct.

I appreciate the opportunity to say publicly that John has made such a difference in Colin's life. From the bottom of our hearts, as parents, both my wife Sarah and I recognize that John gave us the greatest gift anyone can receive. That gift is that Colin now has a future free of the need of prescription drugs and the promise to maximize his human potential.

Colin is now coaching and mentoring young kids in basketball and in life. His passion now is to share what he has learned and experienced from John Gray with as many parents as possible. Colin has helped countless kids and their parents who struggled with many of the issues that he faced. He shares with them the John Gray protocol that changed his life.

For parents who may have children who are struggling with ADD, ADHD, anxiety, depression or other emotional challenges, I would like to say, parent to parent, that what John Gray is offering you is the gift he gave to Colin. His new book *Staying Focused In A Hyper World* can change your child's future just like it has for Colin.

**Drugs for ADHD should be looked at
as the last resort, not the first.**

There are so few times in life, as I said, for a do-over. In my case it was to discover the wisdom of a pioneer who maximized the human potential of children. This is also now for the first time available to you.

There are also few times in history when something so extraordinary is discovered that it will change the world forever.

Staying Focused In A Hyper World will open your eyes to discover that much of what we think about ADD, ADHD, Anxiety and Depression is outdated. I urge you to test out the many suggestions in this book and receive the incredible gift of knowledge that John Gray gave to me more than a decade ago. Do it for your child's future. Give your child the most precious gift of maximizing his or her maximum human potential. I am so honored that John asked me to share Colin's story and to continue this marvelous journey with you.

Peter Greenlaw

Bestselling author *Why Diets are Failing Us, The TDOS Syndrome*™ and *The TDOS Protocol*©

Preface

When talking about brain performance, memory and ADHD, the first question I always get is, "Do you think ADHD is over-diagnosed?" My answer is not a simple yes or no.

Why? Because some people are really asking, "Should we be giving our children all these drugs?"

My answer to that question is a definite NO. Why give your children drugs with dangerous side effects when repeatedly double-blind studies have shown that natural solutions without side effects are more effective? But you probably haven't heard about them.

When asking this same question, other people really mean, "Do think that this condition is real?

To that my answer is a definite YES.

New Trends In Brain Health

Something unprecedented is happening in America and it is gradually spreading around the world. Here is a countdown of new trends regarding brain health, which in turn affect all aspects of our lives and relationships.

Did you know that one out of **ten** American children have been diagnosed with ADHD?[1]

Did you know that one out of **nine** American students seriously contemplate suicide every year?[2]

Did you know that one out of **eight** teenagers suffer from depression?[3]

Did you know that one out of **seven** American women over 55 will develop dementia?[4]

Did you know that one out of **six** American children have a developmental disability?[5]

Did you know that one out of **five** Americans suffer from a mental disorder in a given year?[6]

Did you know that one out of **four** American children have been bullied or attacked?[7]

Did you know that one out of **three** Americans over 70 suffer significant memory loss?[8]

Did you know that one out of **two** Americans over 85 have Alzheimer's disease?[9]

Did you know that in 2013, **one** out 42 American boys were diagnosed with autism spectrum disorder?[10] In 1980 there were only one in ten thousand children diagnosed with autism.

Did you know all of these statistics are increasing every year?[11] Mental illness in America is thirty-five times more common today than thirty years ago.[12]

Do you want to avoid being one of these statistics? Well you can and that is why I wrote this book. At every age and stage of life, brain performance is being challenged for young and old alike. This inhibited brain performance begins with the condition we commonly call ADHD.

Something unprecedented is happening to our brains. It is not only affecting our children but creates new challenges in relationships and marriage. From this perspective, ADHD is actually under-diagnosed.

So, "Is ADHD over-diagnosed?" The answer is not a yes or no. The right answer is "ADHD is overmedicated and under-diagnosed." In the pages that follow, I will prove it to you.

ADHD is overmedicated and under-diagnosed.

In every chapter of *Staying Focused In A Hyper World: Book One*, you will discover a vast array of practical information to increase brain focus, memory and restore love and passion in your life and relationships. You will learn practical insights to heal the one specific condition that gives rise to ADHD and a host of other symptoms that interfere with optimal brain performance. By addressing this one condition, you will have the key to a much more fulfilling future for you and your children.

In *Book One* of the trilogy, we focus mainly on healing the brain to access our full mental and emotional potential. In *Book Two*, we will explore three action steps to develop and express your full potential. In *Book Three*, we will complete the series with an in-depth understanding of super fuel to relax, recharge and sustain your brain power. So lets now take the first step and begin to fully understand and heal ADHD tendencies, improve memory and restore optimal brain performance.

**By addressing one condition,
you can increase brain performance,
improve memory and heal ADHD.**

Simply stated, the biggest obstacle for optimal brain performance is oxidative stress in the brain; by reducing oxidative stress your brain works better. In the most basic terms, oxidative stress occurs when for a variety of reasons there are too many free radicals in the brain and not enough antioxidants to neutralize them.

Most people are not yet familiar with the term oxidative stress and yet there are over 100,000 peer-reviewed studies at the National Institute of Health's website PubMed, which discuss this condition. Brain science can be very complicated but to apply the new discoveries in science to our practical lives it is important that we become aware of the basics. Throughout *Staying Focused In A Hyper World,* we explore the many ways we are unknowingly creating oxidative stress and what we can do to stop it.

Reducing Oxidative Stress In The Brain

Every thought, emotion, and reaction in the brain requires energy. In this process of making energy, free radicals are produced. We cannot avoid free radical production in the brain, but with the right antioxidants we can neutralize these free radicals and prevent oxidative stress.

So what are free radicals and antioxidants? Most simply stated, free radicals are incomplete molecules looking to bond with a stable molecule and antioxidants are special stable molecules with extra electrons to bond with free radicals.

Free radicals and antioxidants work together in various ways to sustain good brain health. This process is a little like dating. Looking for a partner, these incomplete molecules (free radicals) seek out other molecules containing electrons to bond with and live happily ever after. This works out fine as long as there are plenty of antioxidants with extra electrons to bond with.

> **Like the dating process, free radicals**
> **seek out other molecules**
> **containing electrons to bond with.**

Today, blueberries have a rockstar reputation among fruits for fighting cancer and reducing age-related memory loss. Why? Because they are great antioxidants. A bowl of blueberries every other day has proven to dramatically reduce your chances of getting cancer or developing heart disease. According to USDA studies, wild blueberries have the highest antioxidant potential over 20 other fruits. Other studies show that eating blueberries can improve memory, learning and general cognitive function while providing protection against disorders such as Parkinson's disease and Alzheimer's disease.

A blueberry is a great antioxidant because it is both stable and it has an abundance of extra electrons to bond with free radicals. But good foods like blueberries with extra antioxidants are not enough. The body also needs the right nutritional support to make its own more powerful antioxidants. Without enough internally produced antioxidants, free radicals cause oxidative stress, which can then disrupt a living brain cell and inhibit normal brain development and function.

Energy production is not the only cause of free radicals. Every second the brain is being bombarded with extra free radicals caused by nutritional deficiencies, junk food, environmental toxicity, prescribed drugs, and even over-the-counter drugs. If these extra free radicals are not stabilized by an abundance of internally produced antioxidants, then oxidative stress increases.

There are three basic steps to reduce oxidative stress and improve brain function:

1. Decrease our exposure to extra free radicals.
2. Increase our production of antioxidants.
3. Eat more foods rich in antioxidants.

**Oxidative stress results when we have
too many free radicals and too few antioxidants.**

This oxidative stress in the brain gives rise to the symptoms of ADHD in some people, but also a host of other mental symptoms in others like memory loss, depression, anxiety and compulsiveness. This one condition, oxidative stress, inhibits all aspects of brain performance.

The many symptoms of oxidative stress in children go beyond distraction, restlessness and impulsiveness in the classroom.

Eventually, if you live long enough, this same condition leads to dementia, Parkinson's disease or Alzheimer's disease. Amyloid plaque in the brain, which is the result of oxidative stress, is directly linked to memory loss and Alzheimer's disease. This same amyloid plaque is also found to a lesser degree in children diagnosed with autism.

**If you live long enough, ADHD leads to
dementia, Parkinson's disease and Alzheimer's disease.**

The rising statistics measuring ADHD in children are shocking. As mentioned previously, ADHD is diagnosed in 10% of American children. More than half of these children are diagnosed before 6 years old.[13] Many more children have the same oxidative stress but it shows up differently from the standard ADHD symptoms. The oxidative stress in the brain that gives rise to ADHD also gives rise to anxiety disorders, learning disorders, sensory disorders, mood disorders and compulsive disorders. Besides children, adult symptoms of ADHD are also rampant and mostly go undiagnosed.

Almost every client I have helped over 40 years of relationship counseling has had, to some degree, an undiagnosed adult variation of ADHD. You too, may have some degree of ADHD and you don't even know it. Unless pointed out, it may not become obvious to you until your 50s when you can't remember where your car is parked.

To make this book easy reading for most parents who have less time available to them, I have left out detailed descriptions of the studies that support my suggestions and ideas. Instead, I have listed a collection of notes and references in Appendix Six, which link to hundreds of studies and new scientific discoveries for understanding healthy brain function and the many benefits of natural solutions.

**Hundreds of evidence based studies
support natural solutions
for ADHD, memory and focus.**

If you already know you are challenged by ADHD and you just want the bottom line of what to do, I suggest that you read the Introduction and then read Chapter Four, Chapter Ten and Appendix One. That's all you need to begin.

In Chapter Four you will discover fifteen brain drains. They are the hidden causes of oxidative stress. These brain drains prevent your brain from healing. By minimizing your brain drains, the natural solutions in Chapter Ten and Appendix One will be more effective for recharging your brainpower.

Brain drains prevent your brain from healing.

In Chapter Ten, you will be served a buffet of evidence-based natural solutions with double-blind studies to back them up. As you already know, there are always many different ways to achieve a goal. My primary purpose in listing all the options is to reinforce the validity of natural solutions. With so many well-tested options, you will finally have a real choice to go drug-free in your approach to recharge your brainpower. In Appendix One, I provide the protocols that I have found most effective.

With your increased brainpower you can easily go back and read the other chapters. By applying the insights of *Book One* in this trilogy, you will have the basics of restoring normal brain function to access your full potential. In *Book Two* and *Book Three* of the series, we will continue this amazing journey to develop and sustain a lifetime of personal growth and fulfillment.

John Gray, Ph.D.

July 2014

Introduction

One evening after a relaxing dinner together with my wife, I was watching a TV program and she said, "John, your head is shaking."

I was shocked. I had no idea. Everything seemed normal but I had no control over my head movements. When I would focus my mind, my head would involuntarily shake back and forth and I was powerless to control it.

As the days past, the tremors would come and go, but regardless of what I did, they only got worse. When I asked my doctor what I could do, he basically said, "You are just getting old. Don't worry there are good treatments for it."

He went on to gently explain, "You have the early stages of Parkinson's disease."

To me, that felt like a death sentence. After helping to care for my wife's aunt who had Parkinson's disease, I had already learned that the "treatments" he referred to would only temporarily take away symptoms. Over time her condition inevitably got worse until she died.

With most drug treatments, symptoms can be minimized, but over time the condition only gets worse. In the case of Parkinson's disease, as soon as you begin the treatment, the clock begins to tick. Over time you need increasing doses of Parkinson's drugs until they don't work at all and you die. This did not seem like a good plan to me so I began my own research.

Healing Parkinson's Disease

After six months, with the help of many holistic doctors and health researchers, I learned what had caused my condition and how I could heal it with natural solutions. Twelve years later, following a specific healthy protocol of extra nutrition at breakfast, I am still drug-free and symptom free.

Healing Parkinson's disease was in itself a great relief but the outcome of applying the natural solutions I share in this book was much greater than I could anticipate. Not only did the tremors go away but I had become different in ways that I was not expecting.

Once again it was my wife who first noticed. She said, "You have changed. You are like the guy I married." I didn't know what she was talking about but gradually as she explained herself, I understood.

She said, "Since this treatment, you are more relaxed and attentive. When I talk, you don't seem so restless or distracted. After the first few years of marriage, when I talked, it was like you were always in a hurry to be somewhere else. But now you are participating more in our relationship and the family. You are more present."

**"I was always in a hurry
to be somewhere else."**

After taking a moment to reflect on what she was saying, I realized she was right. I had changed. I was more involved in our family activities. I was more present. I thought that she was the one who had changed because she had become happier. Now I knew why.

Besides the changes she noticed in our relationship, I realized that I had much more energy. Most important, I didn't have to push so hard to get things done. Things were easier; my life seemed more orderly and organized.

"Life became easier,
I didn't have to push so hard to get things done."

This was a dramatic change from my prior experience. I noticed that I was not procrastinating or waiting to the last minute to get things done. I could finish projects without needing to feel pressured.

Ever since I was a child, I would wait to the last minute to do things. Sometimes my mother would have to pour water on me to get me out of bed. But, after reversing my Parkinson's disease, this inner resistance I had felt throughout my life was gone. Automatically and almost effortlessly, I could get things done without waiting for a sense of urgency.

I Had ADHD And Didn't Know It

Then it dawned on me. Most of my life, I had ADHD and didn't know it. I just thought life was hard. I had no idea that life could be so much easier; I simply concluded my problems were my problems and I had to just push through them every day. I had no idea that I was experiencing many of the common symptoms of ADHD.

As a student in school, when I focused on learning or reading, I would quickly get tired and often fall asleep. Every day at lunch, I would wake up by eating rolled up balls of white bread without the crust, a pint of milk and several packages of vanilla cookies. The high sugar and gluten content in my lunch would stimulate my brain so that I could feel good and wake up. After school, I would then get my fix of sugar and caffeine with two 16-ounce Cokes. In retrospect, I can now see that I was simply medicating my ADHD with junk food. The stimulation from white bread, sugar and caffeine is the same stimulation one gets from using stimulant drugs for ADHD like Ritalin or Adderall.

**Similar to Ritalin,
sugar medicates symptoms of ADHD.**

Until 1987, when ADHD was first diagnosed, if you were bored and unmotivated, restless and impulsive, or distracted and unable to focus, you just found helpful ways to cope. In those days, we had no idea that these were symptoms that could be healed with natural solutions. Many years later, having healed ADHD, I can now recognize the many symptoms of ADHD that were emerging in my generation while growing up in the fifties and sixties.

As a society, we began to unconsciously feed the rising tide of ADHD with increasing sales of high sugar soft drinks and fast foods, sexual liberation and getting high on drugs and rock and roll. (Not that there is anything wrong with sex and rock and roll.) The point here is that moderation went out the window. Without knowing it, we were medicating our ADHD brains. Parents had no idea that our new coping mechanisms were the result of a brain condition that could be healed.

Although ADHD is a new diagnosis, many of the symptoms of ADHD have been documented for centuries. In my case, it was a severe concussion in the second grade that had caused my condition. I had fallen headfirst from a tree limb two stories high. But today even without concussions, millions of children are exhibiting a wide range of symptoms now identified as ADHD. Never in history have these symptoms been so common in children and adults.

**Never in history have symptoms of ADHD
been so common in children and adults.**

Throughout *Staying Focused In A Hyper World*, we will explore how oxidative stress from environmental toxicity, common over-the-counter drugs, nutritional deficiency and food allergies are inhibiting brain performance in everyone. Symptoms of oxidative stress are now being recognized in children as ADHD, but other symptoms from this same mental condition still go unrecognized. This oxidative stress in the brain gives rise to relationship problems, depression, anxiety and even addictions.

By healing the oxidative stress that was causing my Parkinson's disease, I inadvertently healed my ADHD. It was a surprise discovery; I realized that the same condition that creates ADHD in children also creates Parkinson's disease in seniors. This same condition gives rise to memory loss, dementia or Alzheimer's disease for others.

Healing The Brain

Twelve years ago, I wrote about my journey of healing Parkinson's disease in a book called, *The Mars and Venus Diet and Exercise Solution.* In that book, I explored gender specific insights revealing how diet and exercise can support optimal brain function, weight loss and positive relationships. At that time, I developed a three-month specific protocol of supplements for healing the brain. Since that time I have improved the formula and made it even better. All of the ingredients are easily available online or at health food stores. For your convenience, they are also available at MarsVenus.com/store.

Since that time, studies have been carried out on many of the same ingredients. These studies have proven that specific natural supplements can heal the brain.[1] They have been shown to increase memory, heal ADHD, reverse early stage Parkinson's disease as well reduce or heal anxiety, depression and a host of other mental disorders. Some of the ingredients have even proven to slow down the progression of dementia and Alzheimer's.

**Studies with Parkinson's patients have proven
that specific natural supplements can heal the brain.**

Compared to the *Mars and Venus Diet and Exercise Solution*, the additional insights expressed in *Staying Focused In A Hyper World* can now make your journey to health even more effective and successful. The healthy protocols I suggest, have helped me go beyond just healing Parkinson's disease and ADHD; they have enabled me to consistently access my full mental potential. We all have a greater potential, but to access it, we first need to restore normal brain function, free from the symptoms of ADHD.

**The insights in this book
helped me go beyond healing Parkinson's disease
to creating overall wellness.**

Over the past decade, by sharing my personal experience of healing ADHD, thousands of adults, parents, and children of all ages and stages of life have experienced immediate benefits. With the new insights I will share, increasing memory and healing ADHD is only the first step in a lifelong journey of finding and expressing your inner genius.

In the following chapters, you will discover how to shift from healing the various symptoms of ADHD to developing optimal brain performance. We will explore your potential to shift from a normal life to an extraordinary life.

We will also explore how ADHD shows up differently for men and women in dating relationships and marriage. In many cases, ADHD goes undiagnosed in both men and women because the symptoms also show up differently as we age.

ADHD and Men in Marriage

For married men, an unrecognized symptom of ADHD is the gradual shift of focus from their intimate relationship to their work. Their partners often feel ignored, unappreciated and excluded. ADHD may cause a man to have a kind of tunnel vision or hyper-focus on his work, which in turn decreases his ability to focus on his wife and family.

Jeff and Carol had been married for 10 years. When they came for counseling, Carol was ready to leave the marriage. Carol said, "I know he loves me but I don't feel seen or appreciated. I have tried to make this work but the more I give the less I get. It's like I don't exist for him."

Jeff could not understand why she was upset with him. He said, "I think you are making a big deal out of nothing. I am good provider, I don't argue and I help out around the house more than any of my friends. What else do you want?"

Carol had a long list of complaints but the bottom line was that she felt he had drifted away. He wasn't attentive to her. "You are not interested in me anymore," she said. "You can spend hours on the computer, but when I am talking to you, it's like you are thinking about something else. I can bring you a plate of food and you don't even say thank you or acknowledge me in any way. I don't feel like we are a partnership. I feel like a servant waiting on you. What happened to our love?"

"I do love you," Jeff shared. "I want you to be happy but sometimes it is hard to stay focused on what you are saying. I shift to thinking about problems at work or something else I need to do."

Jeff's symptoms were classic ADHD. But without an understanding of this, Carol took it personally and felt hurt. She felt as though she was alone and everything else was more important than her and her needs.

In coaching, we focused on new listening skills. Jeff was amazed what a difference they made for his wife. As a result he too was feeling much closer to her. Jeff also began my basic protocol of natural solutions to heal his ADHD. As their relationship improved, he shared with me what a difference the supplements had made in all areas of his life.

"My life is so much easier," he said. "It is like I went from a black and white world to full-on Technicolor. I am doing so many more things. And best of all, it is so much easier to listen to Carol. The feelings of connection we had in the beginning are back."

ADHD and the Single Man

For single people, ADHD can interfere with their ability to make a long-term commitment. They come on really strong and then, suddenly and completely, lose all interest. This common pattern is generally not recognized as ADHD.

Steven was 39 and never married. In private coaching, he shared that he was not able to sustain a commitment to one woman. He said, "Every time I get really close to a woman, my feelings change and I lose interest. I am just not turned on. I don't know what happens. Suddenly the grass is greener on the other side of the fence."

For Steven, the challenge and the thrill of the pursuit would turn him on but once he settled down, he would lose the feelings of attraction. He was hot and then cold.

Now lots of therapists would recognize this as a red flag for a fear of intimacy. They would then focus on his unresolved mother issues. In this case, it was such a clear case of ADHD that I just recommended a three-month protocol of natural supplements to heal ADHD and boost his testosterone.

**For single men, ADHD can interfere
with a man's ability to make a long-term commitment.**

We also did about six sessions focusing on his relationship skills and understanding his ADHD. He discovered the addictive behaviors that were continuing to cause his ADHD. This insight motivated him to stop over-exercising and watching Internet porn every day.

"I had no idea that my 'hyper' activities were blunting my ability to feel turned on to my partner," said Steven.

During that time he was able to rekindle his feelings for his current partner and he was able to make a lasting commitment. Prior to his coaching, he had no idea that his problem in making a commitment was ADHD.

"I always thought it was the wrong woman," he told me.

What the Experts
Don't Know and Can't Recognize

Most therapists today are unaware of the adult symptoms of ADHD as well the natural solutions. They do not recognize that ADHD is one of the underlying causes for most relationship challenges. When relationships have problems, counseling or coaching and good communication skills are still needed, but unless the ADHD is corrected, there is less success.

**ADHD is one of the underlying causes
for most relationship challenges today.**

Even some ADHD experts are unaware of how ADHD affects relationships. One night while having dinner with a world-renowned author and expert on ADHD, I mentioned that he too had ADHD. He was surprised and shocked with disbelief.

He replied, "I have no problem with focus. I have so much focus that my wife can be talking to me and I don't hear a word she says because I am so focused on thinking about something else."

I smiled and said, "That's my point. I am sure your wife would agree that you easily become distracted when she begins to talk."

If a well-respected authority on the subject of ADHD did not recognize his own ADHD, I realized at that moment that I needed to write a book about ADHD.

**Even experts don't recognize
all the symptoms of ADHD.**

Millions of adults do not recognize their own symptoms of ADHD because the symptoms may show up differently in different circumstances. Symptoms also change as we age. We will explore how childhood symptoms of ADHD evolve into other adult symptoms. ADHD is not just about restless, distracted or impulsive children unable to sit still in classrooms. That is only the tip of the iceberg.

ADHD and Women in Marriage

Women also have unrecognized symptoms of ADHD. They often become hyper-focused on the needs of others and have difficulty focusing on their own needs. This common expression of ADHD in women results in feeling overwhelmed.

Valerie and Dave had been married for nine years. The passion was gone between them. In coaching, Dave complained, "Valerie is so stressed, no matter what I do it is not enough to make her happy. We don't have fun anymore. She is not even interested in having sex."

ADHD can inhibit a woman's sex drive.

Valerie, like many women today couldn't relax. She said, "I have a million things to do pulling me in different directions. I have no time for me. I feel like I am always trying to catch up. If only I had more hours in the day."

She went on to say, "I don't know why I am not in the mood for sex. I want to relax but I can't. I love Dave and he loves me. But I feel like I have to be there for everyone. If I was to slow down, I might fall apart."

By learning new relationship skills, Valerie was able to overcome this challenge. She learned that sharing her feelings and getting a new kind of support from Dave was essential for lowering her stress levels. By learning to take time for herself, she had more to give to everyone. From my online training *Secrets of Successful Relationships*, Dave learned new skills for listening that made all the difference.

At the same time, they both began my basic protocol for healing ADHD. Valerie also took a few extra supplements for hormone and mood balance. Within a few weeks they were back to having a playful and loving sex life. For women with ADHD, the stress from feeling overwhelmed can inhibit their interest in sex and their ability to enjoy their lives.

In general, ADHD may cause women to focus too much on serving others and less on their own needs. It can also lead to focusing too much on what they don't have instead of what they do have.

ADHD and the Single Woman

For single women, ADHD can give rise to a false sense of independence, inhibiting her interest in an intimate relationship.

By hyper-focusing on what she can do for others, she may disconnect from her own needs for intimacy and relationship. She links her sense of worthiness to what she can do for others and not simply to who she is. In this case, her stress levels continue to rise.

**A woman with ADHD may link
her sense of worthiness to what she can do for others
and not simply to who she is.**

Cindy was an attractive and youthful 45 year old looking for love and divorced for six years. "Why am I invisible to men?" she asked me.

My answer was simple. She was too busy to let a man in her life. She was too independent and didn't really feel the need for a man. By denying this authentic and vulnerable part of her being, she was stressed. A woman can "have it all" but not without support. When a woman is happy, a man is more attracted to her. He senses that he can make her happier and is naturally drawn to her. To a certain extent, a man is always looking for opportunities to make a difference.

**When a woman is too busy,
there is no room for a man in her life.**

She told me, "I don't need a man but I sure would like one." "Needing a man in your life is what makes a woman attractive to a man," I told her. "Sure, you don't need a man to provide for you but you do need a man for you to be happier. You need a man for companionship. You need a man for love and intimacy. Needing a man is not weakness but an invitation for a relationship and an opportunity for him to feel appreciated."

She was surprised and said, "I had no idea, I thought needing someone was a sign of weakness."

For single women, ADHD shows up most commonly as a kind of hyper-independence, but once in a relationship she may feel a kind of hyper-neediness. After years of not needing a man, she may become hyper needy for her partner's affection and reassurance that she is loved. It can also go the other way. When she is hyper-independent, her partner may become needy to connect with her. As a result she loses interest in him. If a woman is seeking to be in an intimate relationship, healing ADHD helps her balance her sense of *independence* with a healthy sense of *dependence* to find a relationship and keep it.

After beginning a three-month course in extra nutritional supplements for ADHD and hormone balance, Cindy slept better and could relax more. She was surprised how quickly she fell in love with a man and started a relationship. As predicted, her neediness began to emerge but with the help of healing her ADHD and learning to take "me-time", it was much more manageable.

Natural Solutions
to Recharge Your Brain Power

In my experience as a relationship counselor and coach, the results are always better when clients support their process of learning with natural supplements. The same nutritional solutions that work for adults also work for children. In many cases, parents whose children have been diagnosed with ADHD or other mental challenges have reported dramatic improvements within days by making a few small changes.

Throughout *Staying Focused In A Hyper World*, we will explore a variety of drug-free, natural solutions, supported by double-blind studies, for healing the brain. In Appendix One, I list a variety of protocols for using these proven drug-free solutions that I have personally used and have witnessed in thousands of children, students and adults to quickly improve brain performance, increase memory and heal the many symptoms of ADHD.

In my experience of helping clients, depending on the cause, there are a variety of natural solutions that may heal the condition. Sometimes the solution is amazingly simple. For example, in children and teens already diagnosed with ADHD, healthy focus is restored and a positive mood is stabilized by replacing breakfast with a super food shake, a good multivitamin, and a few specific supplements.

**Depending on the cause of ADHD,
there are a variety of natural solutions
that may heal the condition.**

I know it seems too good to be true. Yet, for many children, it has helped right away. After all, we are only talking about restoring "normal" brain function. For other children, particularly if they are already taking stimulant drugs or there has been more significant oxidative stress, it takes more time and support.

**Healing ADHD is not that difficult, after all
we are only talking about
restoring "normal" brain function.**

Contrary to what most doctors were taught 10 to 20 years ago (when they went to school), there are now many drug-free, natural solutions for healing ADHD. There has always been and always will be a gap between the most current research and what busy practitioners suggest and prescribe to their patients.

A successful doctor does not have time to stay updated on the most recent research particularly if those solutions are drug-free. In conventional medical schools and in the media, natural solutions are not even part of the ongoing conversation about how to treat ADHD. In the general public, "healing" or "curing" ADHD is not thought to be possible.

**In conventional medical training
"healing" or "curing" ADHD
is not even thought to be possible.**

Using natural solutions for healing ADHD is often minimized as quackery simply because in the past these natural solutions were not backed up with double-blind studies. But now, there are hundreds of well-documented, peer-reviewed, evidence based university studies on the benefits of supplements and special diets. Many of these studies are even double-blind studies. Without an understanding of these real options, parents do not have the choice to go drug-free. With the new insights in *Staying Focused In A Hyper World* you will have a choice.

**Drug-free, natural solutions
need to be part of the
conversation about ADHD.**

Even if you choose to continue using a stimulant drug, you can still use these new insights for brain health to gradually lower the dose and help minimize undesirable side effects. Although I recommend the natural solutions, sometimes the temporary use of stimulant drugs can give a child or an adult a necessary glimpse of normal focus so that they can at least be aware of what they are missing. This glimpse can inspire and motivate them to try the natural solutions that have no negative side effects.

The Many Faces
and Stages of ADHD

Besides providing natural solutions for brain performance, memory and healing ADHD, *Staying Focused In A Hyper World* also provides an in-depth understanding of the many faces, symptoms and stages of ADHD throughout our lives. It is a bigger subject than most people realize. It is not just affecting our children but the entire fabric of our modern society. Unless we are aware of this growing crisis, we are not motivated to seek out and find healing solutions.

**ADHD is not just affecting our children
but the entire fabric of our modern society.**

In the 1800s, while recovering from a devastating Civil War, America became a nation of drunkards. Men drank three times as much alcohol as we do now.[2] In the 1900s, alcohol was slowly replaced by the mass consumption of sugar with even more deadly results. In the 2000s, we are well on our way to a global addiction to stimulant drugs and antidepressants, creating a health care catastrophe.

As mentioned in the Preface, it is estimated that one out of five Americans suffer from a diagnosable mental disorder in a given year.[3] Certainly this increase has to do with more drugs to treat mental illness but as mentioned in the Preface, there is definitely a new trend of increasing mental illness. The drugs prescribed for these disorders can treat symptoms but do not heal the condition. The outcome of using prescribed drugs to treat mental illness is a shocking increase of 35 times more mental illness in just 30 years.[4]

In this century, we are well on our way to a global addiction to stimulant drugs and antidepressants.

Through applying the insights of *Staying Focused In A Hyper World*, this catastrophe can be averted; if not for everyone, at least for you, your family and your circle of friends. I will do my best to share these insights with as many people as I can and hope you will do the same. I have found that most parents are eager to find natural alternatives to giving their children prescription drugs. By sharing these insights you will at least be giving them a choice.

Healing ADHD
is Not Just for Children

Healing ADHD is not just for children. Since I healed my own ADHD twelve years ago, I realized that for adult relationships to thrive, we need more than just new communication skills, we also need the nutritional support necessary for appropriate focus, positive moods and sustained energy. In *Book Two*, we will explore in greater depth how ADHD affects men and women in their relationships.

**For relationships to thrive, we need
optimal brain function.**

In *Book One*, as I explore the causes and solutions for ADHD, when other health challenges linked to brain performance are discussed like allergies, digestion, chronic fatigue, high blood sugar, hormonal imbalance, etc., rather than go off topic, I refer you to MarsVenus.com for additional information. There are over fifty short video blogs exploring natural solutions for a wide range of health challenges. This is to make this book as brief and to the point as possible.

For example, when I talk about balancing blood sugar levels to heal ADHD, the inevitable question of healing diabetes comes up. Not everyone reading this book will be interested in that subject, but some will and I want them to at least know that natural solutions are available.

Rather than simply suggesting they talk with their doctor (which is what most books do), I want to provide them with a real choice. Instead of going into detail regarding a natural solution for diabetes, I provide a link to a free video that explores the issue in greater detail. For example if you have diabetes or you know you have blood sugar issues you could learn more at **MarsVenus. com/blood-sugar**.

Most people do not have a choice to create a healthy life because they are not educated to understand why their body gets sick and what they can do to heal the condition. Many people just assume their family genes determine their sickness and that the drugs provided by their friendly doctors have the power to protect them. I hope to convince you that they don't...but you do. Your genes do not predetermine your sickness and modern drugs cannot protect you.

**Most people do not have a choice
to create a healthy life
because they do not know their options.**

The long-awaited results of the international Human Genome Project have dispelled the myth that genes cause sickness. It is true that our genetic makeup determines the unique ways we get sick but it is our lifestyle choices and environmental conditions that determine if we get sick. The fact that both identical twins in a pair don't develop the same diseases 100% of the time indicates that other factors are involved.[5]

Eating a poor diet or overexposure to toxins first makes you sick and then when you are sick, it activates the genes that give you a heart attack, cancer or diabetes. You can have a cancer gene but it doesn't get activated until you are no longer healthy. With the new knowledge of natural solutions for healing oxidative stress, you have the power to create lasting health in spite of your inherited family genes.

When it comes to ADHD, memory and brain performance, in my experience after sharing these insights with thousands of people, natural solutions can outperform any ADHD drug. In many cases, all it takes is regular exercise, a few extra supplements and a healthy low-carb, nutrient-dense breakfast.

Natural solutions can out perform any ADHD drug.

Breakfast is the most important meal because your brain makes more feel good brain chemicals during the first two hours after sunrise. A bowl of cereal with pasteurized milk, toast and jam or a bowl of oatmeal and a cup of coffee will not do much. But, a cleansing drink, a super food shake and a few supplements can provide the right balance of nutrients essential to heal ADHD. For more information go to **MarsVenus.com/wellness-solution**.

Designing the Right Program for You

Most parents and doctors are just not aware of the natural solutions that can actually heal ADHD. Their solutions are limited to prescription drugs or teaching a child or adult how to "cope" with the disorder. Without this vital insight, the standard debate goes on and on: "Do we use drugs or do we not?"

The answer to this question is not so black and white. We will explore the many options in between. In a few hours, you will have the insights to create the life you have dreamed of. Instead of coping with a condition that could limit you for the rest of your life, you will have the keys to develop and express your full potential for health and happiness.

If you have children and you are reading this book to help them, I suggest you also do it for yourself first. I know it is for your children but it can also be a wake up call for you as well. In my experience, the best way to teach our children is by modeling. We need to first become the change we wish to create.

You can best lead your family by being an example. By noticing the immediate changes in your own ability to focus and manage stress more effectively, you will have the increased confidence necessary to consistently apply these natural solutions for your family.

Staying Focused In A Hyper World is a trilogy of three books. In *Book One*, I will guide you step by step with the necessary insights to first heal the brain to restore normal brain performance and memory. In *Book Two*, we will go further with three action steps to access your full brain and hormone potential for decreasing stress and increasing happiness, passion and vitality. In *Book Three*, I provide the extra nutritional insight to support and sustain your transformation from a normal life to an extraordinary life. We explore the many options for super fuel to relax and recharge your brainpower.

By first exploring and practicing what works best for you, you are paving the way for your children, making their journey as effortless as possible. I have taken twelve years to test these insights with thousands of willing students and now finally get to share these ideas in written form. I hope you enjoy reading this book as much as I have enjoyed writing it.

John Gray, Ph.D.

July 2014

CHAPTER ONE

Focus

Did you know that millions of children and adults today experience a host of new challenges and setbacks because they lack focus?

In epidemic proportions, more children at school are falling behind.[1] At school and at home they are more difficult to manage. But a lack of focus affects all aspects of living.

Without focus, communication breaks down in all relationships and frustration increases. In romantic relationships, passion is lost while breakups and divorce continue to rise.

At work, people are increasingly dissatisfied and bored, often feeling unappreciated, distracted, exhausted or overwhelmed.

Somehow, in the midst of our modern accelerated progress, as a society we have lost our way. In our modern lives, we have a greater consciousness of new possibilities but we have lost our focus.

**We have a greater consciousness
of new possibilities but we have lost our focus.**

The inability to sustain focus on what is most important creates a vacuum in our lives that is automatically filled with a host of unwanted desires, irrational feelings and fears. This lack of focus results in an unconscious denial of what is most important; as if we are lost at sea in a raging storm, we fall prey to a wide range of addictions that rule our lives.

Without focus, our lives lose meaning and purpose, we are easily distracted, forgetting what we are here for: forgetting or never realizing what is most important in life.

Without focus we fall prey to
a wide range of addictions that rule our lives.

This book provides a map to assist you in developing your full potential for creating a fulfilling life. It is not "the" answer but it will help you find "your" answer. It is not filled with helpful philosophies, spiritual insights or self-help tips. Instead, it provides a new understanding of your body and brain to increase your ability to focus.

This new insight can immediately help you apply and integrate the many benefits of education, religion, personal development programs and trainings, counseling, coaching, meditation, biofeedback, EFT, NLP and various other forms of therapy. In addition, these same insights for increasing focus will dramatically improve your health and help free you from dependence on medications for a variety of common health challenges.

Focus is needed in all areas of our lives. It is necessary to finish tasks and get things done. It is an imperative part of communication; it helps us listen more effectively in relationships. It dispels the fog of confusion. It helps us increase our comprehension while reading. But most important, it helps us to hold on to our beliefs and correctly prioritize what is most important.

Focus helps us to hold on to our beliefs
and correctly prioritize what is most important.

Having an MBA (masters of business administration) can certainly help our financial success but for a more fulfilling life we need a MRA (masters of relationship attention.) Without balanced attention and focus, our lives will always be lacking.

For a more fulfilling life we need
a MRA (masters of relationship attention.)

Overall, increasing focus helps us balance and organize our lives properly. It even supports us in developing positive character traits necessary for success and positive relationships, such as patience, persistence, integrity and commitment. The biggest obstacle to achieving healthy focus is now commonly diagnosed as ADHD.

A Short History of ADHD?

In 1980, the name "Attention-Deficit Disorder" was invented by the American Psychiatric Association. In 1987, the name was revised to "Attention-Deficit Hyperactivity Disorder." or ADHD. The official symptoms of ADHD, as diagnosed by doctors, primarily include inattention and/or hyperactivity and impulsivity.

Adults also can have ADHD; up to half of adults diagnosed with the disorder had it as children. As ADHD persists into adulthood, symptoms change. For example, hyperactivity may turn to restlessness; impulsiveness may turn to risk-taking; and distraction may turn to overwhelm. As a result, adults with ADHD often have problems with interpersonal relationships and employment.

ADHD is now the most commonly studied and diagnosed psychiatric disorder in children and adolescents.[2] Addressing this modern challenge, new discoveries about the brain have been made that can benefit everyone at all ages and stages of life. With advanced technology, researchers have found that the brains of children with ADHD are actually different from children without ADHD.[3] It is a real condition.

With advanced technology, researchers have found that the brains of children with ADHD are actually different from children without ADHD.

But medicating this condition with drugs is not the answer. Researchers at the Brookhaven National Laboratory published a study showing that the use of stimulant drugs to treat ADHD changes the brain, making the disorder even worse. Dopamine function in the brain is inhibited by 24%.[4] This change explains why a medical doctor will eventually increase the dosage due to drug tolerance.

Yet, with so much research, there is still much confusion. The term itself prevents many parents and adults from recognizing or relating to this condition. In some ways the term ADHD (Attention-Deficit Hyperactive Disorder) is actually very misleading. The list of common symptoms is often varied and even contradictory and as we will explore later, many symptoms are yet to be defined. While some children are distracted and disorganized, others are restless and impulsive and some are both.

In most cases, there is not an actual deficit of attention at all. Instead, there is an inability to allocate attention appropriately. ADHD children that are inattentive, distracted or "spaced out" are unable to allocate their attention to what their teachers are saying; instead they are focused on a daydream. Other ADHD children that are hyperactive, impulsive or restless are also unable to focus on the teacher but for different reasons. They are simply not that interested in what the teacher is saying. They would rather be somewhere else. They can't sit still in class but they can certainly sit still in front of a TV or video game.

**In most cases of ADHD,
there is not an actual deficit of attention at all.**

Martha Bridge Denckla, M.D., a clinician and scientist at the Kennedy Krieger Institute and Johns Hopkins University, says she faces this confusion regularly from parents who bring their children to the ADHD clinic where she practices. "I am constantly having to explain to parents that ADHD is not a deficit in the sense of say, a budget deficit or a thyroid deficiency, where you don't have enough of something. Rather, it's the control over attention."

The question, Denckla says, is: "Where is the child's attention being allocated? Is it where it needs to be to meet the demands of home, school, and society?

"Allocating one's attention appropriately for success in school requires a degree of willful control—what might be thought of as will power—to turn away from a preferred activity and focus on an activity that may not be as compelling or immediately rewarding."

People with ADHD have plenty of attention – that's why they can still play video games for hours, or get lost in their Legos, or devote endless attention to activities that are biologically more stimulating like junk food, drugs, danger, digital entertainment or internet pornography. They may have plenty of focus but they are unable to easily shift their focus to less stimulating activities.

This inability to focus on less stimulating normal activities causes them to focus more on activities providing extra stimulation. For example, while enjoying the high stimulation of a video game, children are easily distracted from cleaning their room or doing their school homework. Over time, with the increased motivation to play a video game, they disconnect from their inner motivation to cooperate and please their parents and teachers.

Different Symptoms
for the Same Mental Condition

This tendency to focus on those activities that provide immediate and easy gratification, gives rise to an extended range of "hyper" symptoms that show up for different people according to there unique temperaments.

These are a few examples:

- A creative person who likes to start new things becomes hyper-focused on what is new and exciting and is easily distracted from attending to what is routine.
- A responsible person who loves order and loves following rules becomes hyper-controlling and as a result may become oppositional, defiant or simply resistant to change.
- A bold person who is naturally more assertive or action-oriented becomes hyperactive or impulsive. While they mean well, they may easily become inconsiderate of others. They often act or talk without including or considering others.
- A sensitive person who is more vulnerable by nature becomes hyper-vulnerable or moody. Unlike a bold person they may be over-considerate of others. As a result, they become easily hurt when others are inconsiderate of their needs, feelings and wishes.

All of these "hyper" tendencies are symptoms of the same condition that creates ADHD. For simplicity, we will refer to all of them as ADHD. By correcting this tendency we can begin to access increasing degrees of our authentic inner genius potential.

Chapter Two

Natural Solutions for ADHD

Regrettably, new discoveries regarding natural solutions for treating ADHD are overshadowed by outdated medical solutions using stimulant drugs like Ritalin and Adderall. These stimulant drugs have certainly helped many millions of children but they also create undesirable short-term and long-term side effects.[1] The long-term changes are not commonly recognized.

Unless addressed and healed, the brain condition that gives rise to ADHD goes on for a lifetime with many faces and stages. Even stimulant drug manufacturers admit these drugs have repeatedly failed to heal the condition.[2] In treating ADHD, drugs are, at best, limited to temporarily suppressing symptoms because they do not directly address the cause.

No medical studies even suggest that medical drugs can heal the condition that gives rise to ADHD.

The medical community at large continues to be in denial of the abundance of drug-free solutions available today. Universities and mainstream experts usually take a few decades to update their protocols. It is not until better solutions are proven and then demanded by the public that they are finally forced to change.

For example, twenty years ago they did not even consider that changes in diet could prevent and treat diabetes, heart disease and cancer. Yet, health enthusiasts like Paul Bragg, Jack Lalanne and Arnold Ehret have been teaching and applying these insights for the last hundred years.

Many doctors still scoff at natural solutions for health and wellness. Meanwhile, an increasingly large portion of the educated public is wising up, ignoring their doctor's advice and spending billions of dollars each year buying natural supplements and eating organic foods.

In many American hospitals, cancer doctors can lose their jobs or even go to jail for recommending anything other than chemotherapy and radiation.[3] When it comes to medical emergencies, western medicine can save lives, but unfortunately doctors know little about health. Our current system of health care is actually limited to sick care.

**In many American hospitals, doctors
can lose their jobs for
recommending natural solutions.**

I remember just ten years ago when many doctors claimed that sugar and processed foods did not contribute to diabetes, heart disease or cancer. Even today, the sugar industry still promotes the idea that sugar does not cause diabetes.[4] Technically, they are correct; it is not sugar per se but the high amounts of sugar we eat.

Defending sugar is like saying cigarettes don't cause cancer: it is just the daily use of cigarettes that causes cancer. It took fifty years before it was publicly acknowledged by the government that cigarettes cause lung cancer. It will probably be another fifty years before they acknowledge the dangers of holding cell phones to your head.

Today we have slowly progressed to the point where some insurance companies will finally cover non-drug, healing protocols for heart disease. It may take another twenty years before the natural solutions for healing ADHD are recognized by most doctors.

It may take another twenty years
before natural solutions
for ADHD are recognized by most doctors.

With a lack of training in physical, nutritional and behavioral therapy most doctors stick to what they have been taught and know best. To their credit, along with popular media outlets, they have helped identify and increase public awareness of the many symptoms of ADHD so that it can be treated.

Unfortunately, ADHD is still treated with drugs. Diagnosis is often provided to justify giving children and adults potentially dangerous drugs instead of validating a legitimate challenge that can be corrected naturally. Although it is now illegal, in some schools parents were first warned their children might be taken away by child protection services if they refused to give their children drugs to treat ADHD.[5]

ADHD is often diagnosed
to justify giving children drugs
rather than natural solutions.

The use of modern medicines is out of control. Our dependence on drugs rather than education and personal responsibility for our health has created a massive health care crisis. If we continue to medicate our children, the behavior and health challenges we see today will only get worse.

It is my hope that after you read this book and experience the benefit of health education and natural drug-free solutions, you will share these insights with your family, friends and our community. Your successes will inspire others as well. I do not know which solutions will work for you, but I invite you to share your experience at MarsVenus.com.

CHAPTER THREE

What is ADHD?

ADHD is one of the most common neurodevelopmental disorder diagnosed in children and teens.[1] Compared to girls, symptoms of ADHD are twice as common in boys. Data published by the Centers for Disease Control and Prevention reveals that in 2011, one out of five boys and one out of 11 girls were diagnosed with ADHD.[2] Autism, which often goes hand and hand with ADHD, occurs five times more in boys.[3] The CDC reports that one out of 42 boys have ASD (Autistic Spectrum Disorder).[4] This is a shocking and tragic statistic. Just 30 years ago, one in 10,000 children had autism.[5]

ADHD and a spectrum of related mental conditions are a growing epidemic, particularly in America, but it is also spreading around the world. Without practical drug-free solutions, millions of children, teens and adults needlessly spend their lives "coping" with one or more of its hidden undesirable symptoms; from mood disorders and divorce, to obesity, anxiety and addictions.

Without practical drug-free solutions,
we needlessly spend our lives
"coping" with the hidden symptoms of ADHD.

This condition not only touches our children but it affects most adults as well. It causes couples to lose interest and attraction for each other, which eventually leads to divorce. If your ADHD develops into Parkinson's disease, as it did for me, then the odds of experiencing some form of cognitive impairment are one out of two.[6]

The rising tide of dementia and Alzheimer's disease is a mirror to the increasing numbers of children with ADHD. Something new is happening to our brains. This inability to appropriately regulate or sustain focus affects all areas of life at every stage. Without sustained and flexible focus we have limited access to our potential for happiness and success.

**The rising tide of dementia in seniors
mirrors the increasing numbers
of children with ADHD.**

Symptoms of ADHD show up in many different ways but with one common thread. Just add the word "hyper" to almost any normal temperament and you get ADHD. This one condition creates different symptoms that can easily be identified as hyperactive, hyper-focused, hyper-impulsive, hyper-controlling, hypersensitive, hyper-distracted, hyper-introverted, hyper-extroverted, hyper-social, hyper-reclusive, hyper-independent, hyper-passive or simply hyper-spaced-out and unable to focus at all.

**ADHD adds the word "hyper"
to normal temperaments.**

With ADHD, a naturally "introverted child" becomes "hyper" introverted and thus overly fearful of social interactions. A naturally "extroverted child" becomes "hyper" dominant and can be insensitive to others.

Another common difference among children is that some are playful and some serious. A "naturally serious child" becomes "hyper" responsible but often resistant to change and overly judgmental of others.

A "naturally playful child" becomes "hyper" playful and spontaneous to the extent that they don't finish things and become overly disorganized.

ADHD and the Four Temperaments

There can be endless ways to describe and categorize our natural and healthy differences, but to begin a discussion for understanding temperaments we will focus on the four broad categories mentioned in Chapter One. They are "creative," "responsible," "bold," and "sensitive."

In each of these four categories children may also be more analytical, emotional, physical or intuitive. In addition, these categories will commonly show up differently according to natural gender differences, which may be conditioned by social norms and circumstances. ADHD does not determine our temperament but it does alter it.

**ADHD symptoms also vary according
to gender differences,
which are conditioned by social norms.**

Every parent or teacher knows that one child may be more "bold" while another may be more "sensitive." Another child may be a combination of many temperaments. A child's temperament may be similar to a parent's or completely different. In a fluid motion, a child may shift back and forth between many temperaments or simply stay put in one.

With ADHD, a child's natural temperament (or combination of temperaments) becomes chronically exaggerated creating extra challenges and needs. By understanding these distinctions, we can be more accepting and supportive to our children, family members and ourselves. Here are a few examples:

1. Creative Temperament: With ADHD, a child with a creative temperament becomes hyper-focused seeking new stimulation. These happy and playful children have a higher risk of being easily distracted and disorganized. They have difficulty finishing projects and get bored too easily. They can live on the wild side and may be more vulnerable to addictive pleasures. They need extra stimulation, variety and the opportunity to explore different interests. They thrive in the role of student, researcher or problem solver. They seek happiness.

2. Responsible Temperament: With ADHD, a child with a responsible temperament becomes hyper-controlling. These organized and orderly children have a higher risk of being too controlling and critical of others. They can be resistant to change and have difficulty taking risks. They may seek out comfort foods and passive stimulation. They need security, stability and routine. They thrive in the role of judge, organizer or manager. They love order as in "order in the court." They want to be right.

3. Bold Temperament: With ADHD, a child with a bold temperament becomes hyper-assertive. These busy and highly motivated children have a higher risk of being inconsiderate or mean to other children. They can go too fast, acting or speaking without thinking of consequences. To avoid feeling bored, they can be thrill seekers. Danger is their game. They are more vulnerable to addictive substances. They need extra acknowledgment for what they do, and increased opportunities to feel successful in making a difference. They thrive in the role of leader, boss or protector. They seek power.

4. Sensitive Temperament: With ADHD, a child with a sensitive temperament becomes hyper-vulnerable. These caring and considerate children have a high risk of feeling depressed, anxious, unhappy and over-emotional. In the absence of feeling nurtured, they may unconsciously seek out negative attention. They need extra empathy and attention to their feelings. They also need to feel helpful and emotionally supportive to others in need. They thrive in the role of nurturer, supporter and team player. They seek to be good.

The oxidative stress that gives rise to ADHD does not determine our natural differences in temperament but it does cause imbalance. ADHD is simply another way of saying a chronic imbalance in brain function that exaggerates our natural tendencies.

Changing Temperaments

A child or adult without ADHD may easily shift from one temperament to another depending upon circumstances. Every person tends to have a dominant temperament that comes forth when they feel safe to be themselves. Then, when they feel supported, another may come forth. At other times, when they feel challenged and need extra support, they shift to another. And finally, when they feel needed, another comes forth. These are a few examples:

1. Creative Temperament: When people with a creative temperament feel supported, they may become more responsible and finish things. When they feel challenged, they may shift to becoming more sensitive and caring. When they feel needed, they may shift to becoming more bold and expressive.

2. Responsible Temperament: When people with a responsible temperament feel supported, they may become bolder and willing to take more risks. When they feel challenged, they may shift to become more flexible and creative. When they feel needed, they may shift to becoming more compassionate and sensitive.

3. Bold Temperament: When people with a bold temperament feel supported, they may shift to become more caring and sensitive. When they feel challenged, they may shift to become more authoritative and responsible. When they feel needed, they may shift to becoming more creative.

4. Sensitive Temperament: When people with a sensitive temperament feel supported, they may become more playful and creative. Sometimes all they need is a good cry and then suddenly they feel happy and carefree. When they feel challenged, they may shift to become more confident and bold. When they feel needed, they may shift to becoming more responsible and accountable.

In this way, people generally have one dominant temperament but shift between secondary temperaments when they feel supported, challenged or needed.

ADHD and Changing Temperaments

The oxidative stress associated with ADHD, not only causes normal temperaments to become hyper or magnified but it also makes shifting back and forth between the temperaments more difficult. In the following four examples we will explore how ADHD inhibits the natural flow of one temperament to another according to circumstances and situations.

1. ADHD and the Creative Temperament: With ADHD, even when they feel supported, it becomes difficult for the focused hyper-creative child to shift temperaments and become more responsible. Instead, they become the opposite of more responsible; they become forgetful, scattered and disorganized. If challenged, instead of becoming more sensitive, they become completely and unintentionally indifferent to others. When needed instead of becoming more bold and motivated to serve others, they become unproductive, overly cautious and resistant to taking risks. They will tend to wait until the last minute to do things. Think of the creative writer who spends years never finishing his book or the artist who doesn't want to sell his or her work.

2. ADHD and the Responsible Temperament: With ADHD, even when they feel supported, it becomes difficult for the compulsive hyper-responsible child to shift temperaments and become more assertive or bold. Instead, they become the opposite of more bold: they become overly cautious and resistant to change. If challenged, instead of becoming more creative, they become uninspired and unimaginative. When needed, instead of becoming more sensitive to the needs of others, they become cold as ice; sternly or strictly adhering to the rules or law. Think Judge Judy when her buttons get pushed.

3. ADHD and the Bold Temperament: With ADHD, even when they feel supported, it becomes difficult for the impulsive hyper-bold child to shift temperaments and become more sensitive to the needs and feelings of others. Instead, they become the opposite of more sensitive: they become insensitive, indifferent or arrogant. If challenged, instead of becoming more responsible to do the right thing, they become impatient, impulsive and irresponsible; taking too many risks. When needed, instead of becoming more creative and motivated to solve problems, they become easily bored and unmotivated to do anything, unless they "have to" or it is a big emergency. They are easily addicted to watching sports or playing video games. Think Superman at work and couch potato at home.

4. ADHD and the Sensitive Temperament: With ADHD, even when they feel supported, it becomes difficult for the vulnerable hypersensitive child to shift temperaments to become more flexible and creative. Instead, they become the opposite of more creative: they become inflexible or fixed. They resist all support or good advise. "Yes, but" is their automatic response. If challenged, instead of becoming more bold and assertive, they become more fearful and defensive. They focus on what they don't want, instead of what they do want. When needed, they tend to focus more on what they are not getting and, as a result, give less. Think Ebenezer Scrooge.

In all of these examples, by healing ADHD and restoring normal dopamine function we automatically return to our normal temperaments and freely shift between them as is appropriate to the circumstance or situation.

Chapter Four

What Causes ADHD?

Some say bad parenting causes ADHD. Others say it is the genes.[1] But bad parenting or bad genes have been around for thousands of years and we have not had an epidemic of ADHD. Our genes determine our unique temperament but something else causes the "hyper" condition we call ADHD.

Parenting styles can certainly support or inhibit the health of a child, but styles have not changed that much and they don't cause ADHD. Normal parenting styles can condition the brain but they do not necessarily produce oxidative stress in the brain. Children have ADHD regardless of whether their parents are strict or permissive. Unless a parent is physically or emotionally abusive, they certainly don't cause oxidative stress.

Parenting styles have not changed that much and they don't cause ADHD.

There are also those who minimize the epidemic of ADHD saying it is overdiagnosed to justify selling more drugs to children.[2] It is true that we are becoming a society that is overly dependent on drugs for every condition, but the fact remains that millions of people are suffering from the symptoms I have described in this book.

**Some people minimize the epidemic of ADHD
saying it is over-diagnosed
to justify selling more drugs to children.**

Those who have not experienced the paralyzing effects of anxiety, procrastination, brain fog or sleepless nights can have no conception or empathy for how ADHD is affecting millions of children and adults. What they fail to recognize is that their lack of empathy and compassion is in itself a form of ADHD and they too could benefit from recognizing the many faces of ADHD and its many causes.

**A lack of empathy for those with ADHD
is actually another symptom of ADHD.**

Others claim that ADHD is merely psychological and not a physical impairment of the brain.[3] They conclude drugs are not the answer but that counseling alone can heal the condition. Counseling or some form of emotional support should always be part of the equation for healing the brain but the cause of ADHD is definitely not just "psychological" nor is the solution.

Modern brain scans can now detect clear differences in the ADHD brain verses the non-ADHD brain.[4] ADHD is not just laziness or an excuse for poor performance. It is not just in the "head" but it is literally in the brain. It is now proven to be a measurable physical impairment of normal brain function caused by oxidative stress.

**ADHD is not just in the "head"
but it is literally in the brain.**

The rise of ADHD, bipolar and autism is clearly the result of something new that we, as a society, have started doing in the last thirty years. Listed below are fifteen different changes common in our modern lifestyle. These changes contribute to or directly cause oxidative stress. This increase in oxidative stress, both in the gut and brain, gives rise to the symptoms of ADHD.

Oxidative stress, both in the gut and brain, gives rise to the symptoms of ADHD.

By addressing the real cause of ADHD, you can recharge your brainpower. In the simplest of terms, as discussed in the Preface, the cause of ADHD is oxidative stress in the brain. By healing this condition, we heal ADHD.

In Chapters Nine through Thirteen, we will explore the natural solutions for healing ADHD but first we must understand the many hidden causes of oxidative stress. Natural solutions can be most effective if we first stop causing oxidative stress.

The Many Causes of Oxidative Stress

A concussion or shock to the body is an obvious cause of oxidative stress in the brain, but there are a multitude of other, often unrecognized, ways. The fifteen most devastating causes of oxidative stress are:

1. Acetaminophen: Fever suppressants, cold, flu, allergy and pain relief pills like Tylenol, Nyquil, Percocet and Vicodin, which contain acetaminophen contribute to the oxidative stress that gives rise to ADHD. Tylenol, the biggest selling over-the-counter medicine in the world, has only been widely used since 1980, which is when ADHD, bipolar and autism began to increase. Over 600 hundred medicines contain the active ingredient acetaminophen.

Acetaminophen inhibits the natural production of glutathione, which is produced by your liver to protect the brain from free radical oxidation.[5] The result is oxidative stress. When used to suppress fevers, this commonly used medicine suppresses your brain's natural ability to defend and heal itself.[6] A 2014 study in JAMA Pediatrics revealed that children whose mothers took acetaminophen while pregnant had a 40% higher risk of being diagnosed with ADHD.

Acetaminophen inhibits the
production of glutathione,
which is necessary to protect the brain from oxidative stress.

Children and adults with ADHD, bipolar and autism, as well those who suffer from dementia, Parkinson's disease and Alzheimer's disease, have low glutathione production.[7] Low glutathione levels also inhibit the growth of the myelin sheath. The myelin sheath insulates your nerves and protects the brain from overstimulation. "Demyelination" caused by oxidative stress in the brain is the hallmark of neurodegenerative disease. Demyelination is just another way of saying oxidative stress.

In *Book Two* of this series, we will explore in much greater detail the link between acetaminophen, vaccinations and autism. It is the acetaminophen in Tylenol that allows vaccinations and other medications to trigger chronic oxidative stress in the brain resulting in a host of life-long mental challenges. In Cuba, Tylenol is greatly restricted and, as a result, children don't become autistic after taking vaccinations.

2. MSG: Chronic exposure to known neurotoxins like MSG (monosodium glutamate) and HVP (Hydrolyzed Vegetable Protein) make the brain more vulnerable to the free radical oxidation caused by mercury.[8] Mercury is most commonly found in fish due to bioaccumulation. Mercury is ingested by smaller fish that are in turn ingested by larger fish. Each time a larger fish consumes a smaller fish their levels of mercury increase. Thus the largest fish contain the highest amounts of toxic mercury. Taking supplements with selenium can neutralize mercury and reduce oxidative stress.

Big fish contain the highest
accumulation of toxic mercury.

Mercury is also found in non-organic foods, dental amalgam fillings and the air we breathe and the water we drink. Major contributors to emissions of mercury are car exhaust, coal-fired electrical power plants, and hospitals with medical waste incinerators. Children, pregnant women and women of child bearing age are most vulnerable to the effects of mercury.

ADHD and dementia both share one common denominator: they can be triggered by heavy metals like mercury.[9] Unfortunately MSG and HVP are approved by the FDA. MSG is not just in Chinese food but it is added to thousands of packaged foods.

Unfortunately MSG and HVP
are approved by the FDA.

Manufacturers are not required to put MSG on the label: instead they can simply say "natural flavors". What is more tragic is that many baby formulas also include MSG. For more sensitive children, MSG and a host of other chemicals added to processed foods can be directly responsible for ADHD.

3. Sugar: High blood sugar levels cause oxidative stress in the brain.[10] The excessive consumption of soft drinks, fruit juice, bread, cookies, chips, ice cream, cakes, pudding, etc. elevate blood sugar levels. High blood sugar levels contribute to ADHD by causing oxidative stress in brain neurons and chronic inflammation throughout the brain.

**High blood sugar levels cause
oxidative stress to brain neurons.**

High blood sugar levels in mothers during pregnancy can over-stimulate a developing baby's brain causing a decrease in dopamine receptor sites. This down regulation of dopamine receptors (due to high sugar levels) has been linked to ADHD.[11] Mothers in the future will avoid high-carb junk foods just as mothers today avoid alcohol and smoking.

In addition, high insulin levels, which result from high blood sugar levels, inhibit glutathione production making the baby's brain more vulnerable to oxidative stress by toxic metals like lead, mercury and aluminum.[12] Pregnant mothers should particularly avoid lipsticks and other cosmetics which are known to contain both lead and aluminum.

Toxic metals are linked to a variety of mental disorders. Violence and criminal behavior is directly linked to lead poisoning in the brain.[13] ADHD is linked to high mercury levels in the brain.[14] Alzheimer's disease and dementia are linked to high aluminum levels in the brain.[15] All of these conditions are also linked to low glutathione levels. Increased glutathione production is needed to remove these toxic heavy metals.

**Violence and criminal behavior
is directly linked to lead poisoning in the brain.**

Numerous research studies link sugar consumption to the symptoms of ADHD.[16] They postulate that sugar acutely increases dopamine, which over time leads to a reduction in dopamine receptors. This downregulation of dopamine receptors causes ADHD. Children with ADHD will then ingest more sugar in an attempt to compensate for inhibited dopamine function.

4. Unfermented soy and pasteurized dairy: ADHD can be caused by inhibited digestion due to consuming soy protein, soy milk and pasteurized dairy products. Most fast food hamburgers are also supplemented with indigestible soy products. Baby formulas with soy protein or pasteurized dairy protein also inhibit digestion. Inhibited digestion prevents the production of metabolic enzymes and amino acids necessary for healthy brain function. It's important to note that "fermented" soy products and raw dairy products are not harmful and do not cause inhibited digestion.

**Baby formulas with soy protein
or pasteurized dairy protein inhibit digestion.**

5. Sedentary Lifestyle: Our sedentary lifestyle prevents lymphatic circulation to detoxify the brain of heavy metals, chemicals and toxins in our air, water and food. This increased toxicity causes brain infections and inflammation.

Lack of exercise prevents brain cell growth and limits blood circulation to heal brain infections. Physical movement is necessary for brain development and the production of neurotransmitters in the brain. Without enough neurotransmitter production, instead of exercise we seek out forms of passive stimulation to avoid the feelings of boredom associated with low production of brain chemicals. This passive stimulation feels good but it does not support brain development and growth.

6. Stress: Chronic psychological stress induced by excessive punishment, loss, disapproval, violation or threat raises stress hormones, which in turn cause oxidative stress in the brain. The chronic production of stress hormones inhibits the production of glutathione, which is your body's master molecule for minimizing oxidative stress. Various forms of childhood or adult trauma can raise your cortisol set point, which in turn sustains higher blood sugar levels causing even more oxidative stress in the brain.

Oxidative stress in the brain is amplified at this time in history because sugar and caffeine products are so widely consumed. As mentioned before, high blood sugar levels are a known neurotoxin causing brain cell death and increasing levels of oxidative stress. Excessive caffeine, particularly when combined with sugar, over-stimulates dopamine production in the brain. This high dopamine stimulation eventually leads to addictive tendencies, oxidative stress and ADHD behaviors.

Oxidative stress in the brain is amplified
because sugar and caffeine products
are so widely consumed.

Caffeine tends to spike stress hormones yet studies on caffeine users have indicated a decreased risk of Parkinson's disease and cognitive decline when high dose caffeine users are compared to low dose caffeine users and non-users. A high dose is four or more cups of coffee a day. Regular caffeine used at high doses can reduce one's cravings for sugar, reduce insulin resistance and minimize excessive sugar consumption. In this respect, caffeine use without sugar can protect the brain from oxidative stress.

High dose caffeine users are healthier than sugar users but not necessarily healthier than those who have no caffeine and have low sugar consumption. That is why coffee is not recommended for health but if one does choose to drink coffee, it is best to avoid the sugar. Caffeine is also known to reduce serotonin levels in the brain, which adversely affects people who are naturally more sensitive. Research studies reveal that women are more vulnerable to low serotonin levels than men.

The effects of oxidative stress
are amplified due to
high sugar and caffeine consumption.

I personally enjoy coffee when I need a little extra lift but I make sure that I am not dependent on it. In France, one generally has coffee or tea after a dessert. This extra caffeine helps the body to absorb the sugar in the dessert and prevents a spike in blood sugar. For those who enjoy coffee and do not experience some of the common side effects like addiction, headaches, sedentary lifestyle, hypertension, gout, incontinence, insomnia, indigestion, jitteriness or nausea, it is much better than the high sugar diet so many people are addicted to.

High stress levels during pregnancy or during the birthing process combined with high blood sugar levels in the mother can definitely contribute to ADHD in children.

7. Stimulant Drugs: A myriad of brain scans have proven that excessive dopamine stimulation due to street drugs like cocaine, crack, heroin and methamphetamines change and injure the brain.[17] Similar changes take place in the brain when taking prescribed stimulant drugs for ADD and ADHD.[18]

Ritalin, a commonly prescribed ADHD drug, and cocaine act in the brain through the same pathways. Adderall, which is slightly different, acts in the brain in a way similar to methamphetamines or crystal meth. Fifty to sixty percent of college kids take Ritalin or Adderall.[19] Thirty to fifty percent of adolescents in drug rehab centers have used Ritalin.[20]

Stimulant drugs can have a big effect on the brain from just the first use. A new study at UC San Francisco's Ernest Gallo Clinic and Research Center has revealed that cocaine may rewire the brain and drastically affect decision-making after just one use. This change makes the search for extra stimulation override other priorities.[21]

**Stimulant drugs
make the search for extra stimulation
override other healthy priorities.**

A report published in 2005 by neurologist George A. Ricaurte and his team at the Johns Hopkins University School of Medicine is even more "damning" to ADHD meds.[22] Ricaurte's group trained baboons and squirrel monkeys to self-administer an oral formulation of amphetamine similar to Adderall. "Two to four weeks later the researchers detected evidence of amphetamine-induced brain damage, encountering lower levels of dopamine and fewer dopamine transporters on nerve endings in the striatum."

**Even low dose stimulant drugs have
repeatedly shown to increase
oxidative stress in the brain.**

According to Professor William Carlezon of Harvard University, ADHD medication damages the nucleus accumbens in the developing brain leading to a loss of drive in adulthood.[23] This research was confirmed by research at Brown University, University of Michigan, University of Pittsburgh, South Carolina, and universities in Holland, Sweden, Italy and the Netherlands.[24]

Each study found damage to the nucleus accumbens even when low doses were given for a short period of time. The nucleus accumbens in the brain is important for motivation, focus, pleasure, interest and even falling in love. It regulates the production of feel good brain chemicals like dopamine and serotonin.

Oxidative stress to this area of the brain is not only associated with addictive cravings and behaviors but with ADHD as well. From this evidence-based perspective, addictions are simply one of the ways a person seeks to temporarily reduce or eliminate the symptoms of ADHD. While these researchers confirmed the injury to be permanent, they have not yet studied the effects of natural solutions to assist the brain in healing this condition.

8. Video Games: As with all activities that produce huge profits, to suggest they are harmful in some manner is going to be controversial. The Wall Street Journal reports, "A growing body of research suggests that "gaming" improves creativity, decision-making and perception, improved hand-eye coordination and improved vision for discerning gray tones."[25] People who play video games can make decisions 25% faster. A popular TED talk also reinforces the many benefits of violent video games.

While this sounds amazing, anyone who takes a stimulant drug like cocaine, caffeine or methamphetamines (speed) will also experience improved memory, increased creativity and faster decision-making abilities. Violent video games like stimulant drugs will temporarily improve ADHD symptoms. Like drugs, however, they will also create long-term brain injury. Playing violent video games has a similar effect on the brain as taking any stimulant drug including doctor prescribed Ritalin or Adderall.

**Benefits from video games abound
but like taking stimulants drugs
there are negative side effects.**

Just because playing video games increases creativity, it doesn't mean they are good for you. A variety of harmful drugs also increase creativity. And just like taking drugs, video games have side effects. It is common knowledge in entertainment circles that many creative writers, composers and entertainers have a history of depending on drugs or alcohol for stimulation and motivation. The number of Hollywood stars who are always going to "rehab" is a testament to drug addiction and creativity. Here is a partial list from some well-known names in history:

- Charles Dickens used opium.
- Nobel Prize winner Ernest Hemingway and Edgar Allan Poe were both known to be addicted to alcohol.
- Reclusive Howard Hughes injected himself with opiates.
- Marilyn Monroe was addicted to barbiturates.
- The Russian composer Tchaikovsky was addicted to alcohol.
- One of the top grossing actors in history, Robert Downey Jr. has admitted to smoking crack, trying heroin and pretty much every other drug under the sun.
- Sigmund Freud was a great proponent of cocaine and used it to treat his depression.
- Jimmy Hendrix, members of the Beatles, Jim Morrison of the Doors and most other rock stars during the 60's were composing and performing under the influence of a variety of drugs.
- Bestselling writer Stephen King said he used a huge cocktail of drugs to assist him in writing. He used cocaine, Valium, Nyquil, beer, tobacco and marijuana.
- Vincent van Gogh was an alcoholic, and eventually shot himself.
- Winston Churchill was known to stay up taking amphetamines.

- Thomas Edison was known to regularly consume cocaine-laced elixirs.
- Steve Jobs said experimenting with LSD in the 60's was one of the most important things he had done in his life.
- Preeminent astrophysicist Carl Sagan smoked marijuana regularly.
- Lenny Bruce, one of the godfathers of modern stand-up comedy, was a drug addict and eventually died from an overdose.
- John Belushi a creative comedy icon from Saturday Night Live died from a drug overdose. The list goes on and on of comedians who regularly use cocaine and marijuana.

Playing a video game improves hand-eye coordination but so does throwing a ball. As with any activity, practice makes perfect. When it comes to extended video game play, the benefits are there but so are the side effects. There are much healthier ways to recharge the brain to improve its performance.

Playing a video game improves hand-eye coordination but so does throwing a ball.

Video games change your brain but so does reading, playing the piano, listening to music, or even navigating your car and there are no negative side effects. Researchers found that London cab drivers have a uniquely bigger hippocampus than almost anyone else.[26] The four-year process of learning to navigate the streets of London actually increases the size of the brain called the hippocampus, which has to do with memory. When a London cab driver retires, these changes shrink back again, confirming the common wisdom, "use it or lose it."

Research confirms that video games like other challenging activities certainly create positive changes in the brain but these studies overlook the real danger of video games. A moderate use of video games, like any fun activity, is not a problem. Excessive use, however, particularly video games involving violence, is like taking a stimulant drug, which causes oxidative stress.

**Excessive use of video games
involving violence is like taking a stimulant drug
that causes oxidative stress.**

Researchers at Indiana University using brain scans reported that playing violent video games alters brain function in healthy young men after just a week of play, depressing activity among regions associated with emotional control.[27] Other studies have found an association between compulsive gaming and being overweight, introverted and prone to depression.[28]

To understand this dark side of video games, lets review what we have learned about ADHD and drugs. A stimulant drug floods the brain with higher than normal levels of dopamine. This over-stimulation causes dopamine receptor sites to downregulate causing a dependence on the stimulant. In the case of video games, this stimulation increases blood flow to the "nucleus accumbens" or pleasure center in the middle of the brain. At the same time blood flow decreases to the prefrontal cortex.[29] Activity in the prefrontal cortex is associated with decision-making and control over impulses.

Extended time on a video game increases our ability to play the game but decreases our control over automatic impulses.[30] To a lesser degree watching TV, listening to loud music, junk food and modern bread have a similar effect on the nucleus accumbens.

**Extended time playing a video game
decreases our control over automatic impulses.**

A recent brain imaging study by researchers at Stanford's school of medicine suggests that men are more vulnerable to addiction to video games.[31] Up to 90 percent of American youth play video games and as many as 15 to 31% percent (more than 5 million kids) may be addicted. Boys are three times more likely than girls to feel addicted to video games.

The neural circuitry that mediates desire for internet video games is similar to that observed with substance dependence.[32] With excessive stimulation, this middle area of the brain becomes desensitized and is less affected by normal stimulation. This causes the number one symptom of ADHD: boredom in response to normal stimulation and the increased need to escape boredom through excessive stimulation.

**Video games cause increased
boredom in response to normal stimulation.**

In practical terms, this means the opportunity to play a video game, watch TV or eat a dessert becomes more important to the child than the normal stimulation of doing what it takes to earn the approval of a parent or teacher. In addition, the decreased activity of the prefrontal cortex inhibits our ability to sustain focus on what is most important. While boys often loose their motivation in school, girls become overly motivated to please the teacher at the expense of their own needs.

9. Induced Labor: Induced birthing procedures using synthetic oxytocin (Pitocin) have proven to double the risk of ADHD. In a study of 300 children whose mothers received Pitocin at birth to induce labor, 67.1% of the children were diagnosed with ADHD.[33] Induced labor has also been linked to autism. A study in North

Carolina reported that women whose labor was induced were 16% more likely to have a child later diagnosed with autism.[34]

While induced labor can sometimes save lives, it is overused simply to make the birthing process more convenient for doctors and hospitals. Twenty-five percent of mothers in the US receive Pitocin during labor.[35] In some hospitals up to ninety percent of mothers receive Pitocin.[36]

Mothers who treat their own ADHD symptoms with natural solutions are able to produce an abundance of their own oxytocin to induce natural birth.[37] Research reveals that healthy production of neurotransmitters is directly associated with the release of oxytocin.[38] By learning to naturally increase oxytocin levels the need for synthetic oxytocin to induce birth is not necessary. For more information on natural solutions to increase oxytocin read *Why Mars and Venus Collide* or *Venus On Fire, Mars On Ice.*

10. Divorce: Statistics reveal a greater risk of ADHD in children of divorced parents, particularly when boys are missing the regular influence of their fathers or their mothers are unable to find happiness.[39] The presence of a father figure increases the brain chemical dopamine in a child while the presence of a happy mother can also generate healthy levels of this brain chemical.[40]

Dopamine is the brain chemical for focus and motivation. ADHD is directly related to inhibited dopamine function. The stress of divorce combined with other factors that contribute to oxidative stress can easily cause ADHD.

11. Pornography: A 2006 Dutch study found that erotica had the highest addictive potential of all internet applications.[41] A study using brain scans at Cambridge University found that pornography addiction leads to the same brain activity as alcoholism or drug abuse.[42]

Online pornography and non-personal sex can stimulate massive dopamine levels, and like any addictive drug, this intense increase of dopamine will change the brain by downregulating dopamine receptors. This downregulation requires increased stimulation to provide normal levels of sexual fulfillment.

Internet porn is like heroin to the brain.

During normal intimate sexual intercourse, the body releases four times more prolactin than from masturbation.[43] This increased prolactin is associated with sexual satiety in both men and women. It is a natural "I'm done" signal. The low prolactin levels associated with masturbation or "internet porn" provide the unique ability to override this natural signal. As a result, internet porn can lead to a blunting of interest in sex with a real partner and an increased desire for more porn.[44]

12. Antibiotics, Pesticides, Plastics and GMOs: Antibiotics kill dangerous bacteria in the gut but it is also well known that they kill good bacterial as well. The absence of good bacteria allows a toxic fungus called candida to overpopulate the gut. Although it is still not commonly accepted by mainstream medicine, holistic health practitioners recognize that children with ADHD and autism almost always have different degrees of indigestion caused by an excess of candida.[45] Taking probiotics after the use of antibiotics is one way to help avoid this outcome.[46]

Excessive candida in the gut inhibits the healthy production of B vitamins and neurotransmitters necessary for normal brain performance. Without the ability to make B12, the liver is unable to make the glutathione needed to protect the brain from oxidative stress. Children who were not breastfed, or have taken lots of antibiotics, have a higher risk of bowel disease and candida infestations.[47]

**Constipation and other bowel conditions
are directly related to ADHD.**

Both genetically modified foods (GMOs) or the residue of pesticides in non-organic foods will also kill off beneficial bacteria in the gut and give rise to excessive candida and gut problems. GMO foods contain toxic doses of the herbicide glyphosate. Studies have already confirmed that glyphosate alters and destroys beneficial intestinal bacteria in animals.[48] When we eat meat from animals fed GMOs, it also destroys the good bacteria in our intestines.

Common GMOs fed to animals are corn, soy and alfalfa. Unless they are labeled organic, the following foods in the grocery store are most likely GMOs: they are corn, corn syrup, beets, sugar, yellow squash, zucchini, papaya, pineapple, Canola oil and all dairy products. In addition many packaged foods and breads contain GMO additives that have been produced by GMOs. When you shop, there are still many non-GMO options. You can find a free non-GMO Shopping Guide at http://www.nongmo-shoppingguide.com/download.html. If foods are labeled organic, then they are not only pesticide-free but also GMO-free.

Foods labeled organic are GMO-free.

GMO glyphosate is also directly linked to ADHD and dopamine function because studies reveal that it inhibits the utilization of the amino acids phenylalanine, tryptophan and tyrosine.[49] Phenylalanine is necessary to make tyrosine, which in turn makes dopamine. Tryptophan is the amino acid necessary to make Vitamin B3, which balances cholesterol, increases energy production and is necessary for blood circulation to the brain. Tryptophan is also needed to make the calming brain chemical serotonin. Deficiency of serotonin is directly linked to higher stress levels, anxiety and depression. The inhibition of tyrosine is linked to weight gain, low metabolism and inability to focus.

Eating foods that are genetically modified (GMOs) is directly linked to ADHD.

One the biggest problems caused by GMO glyphosate is oxidative stress. Every second, energy production in the brain and body is producing millions of free radicals. The brain's natural defense against oxidative stress is glutathione. Glyphosate impairs the transport of sulfate for the liver to make glutathione.[50] In addition, glyphosates inhibit both the production of key hormones and vitamin D.[51] Vitamin D production and utilization is essential for over 2000 genes and a key player in brain development.

Besides gut problems, children with ADHD have hormonal imbalances, which can be directly caused by exposure to synthetic chemicals. In 2003, scientists discovered that the popular pesticide "Endosulfan" blocks the action of testosterone in boys which in turn disrupts and delays the process of puberty.[52] In addition, healthy dopamine function and motivation, particularly in boys, is directly related to testosterone. A 2007 study by the California Department of Public Health found that women who lived near farm fields sprayed with Endosulfan during the first eight weeks of pregnancy are several times more likely to give birth to children with autism.

Popular pesticides disrupt the production of important hormones and brain chemicals.

Endosulfan is still commonly used, but as of July 2010 the Environmental Protection Agency has initiated action to gradually end its use in United States by July 31, 2016. After 20 years and many lawsuits, the EPA finally reports that it is being discontinued "because it can pose unacceptable health risks to farm workers and wildlife and can persist in the environment." It is still being used in many countries around the world from where Americans import food.

Atrazine, the most common pesticide used in America, is now banned in Europe. Studies from University of California, Berkley have shown that when a small amount of Atrazine is added to water, it causes male frogs to grow female ovaries.[53] US farmers use about 27,000 tons of Atrazine to protect corn and other crops from weeds. The chemical compound blends with rain, groundwater, rivers and streams. Eight sites were tested from Iowa to Utah and researchers found up to 92% of male frogs had abnormal testicles with extra female ovaries.

Due to common pesticides in the water,
up to 92% of male frogs
had abnormal testicles with extra female ovaries.

Another major hormone disruptor for both boys and girls is plastics. Due to the increasing use of plastics, girls are showing signs of puberty earlier than normal and boys are experiencing delayed puberty by a couple of years.[54] In the last decade, scientists have discovered that plastic bottles, pacifiers and baby bottles, as well as a host of soft drink plastic bottles, contain high levels of toxic BPA and "phthalates" (the "ph" is silent.) In 2005, a team of researchers at the University of Cincinnati published research to show that these phthalates, which leach out of plastic bottles or liners used in baby bottles, irreversibly disrupt brain development in laboratory animals.

Phthalates from plastic have been
found to disrupt brain development.

In 2004, neuroscientists identified a crucial link between hormone disruptors and ADHD.[55] When young laboratory animals were exposed to a variety of hormone disruptors, including phthalates, they oxidized parts of the brain. These laboratory animals became quite "hyper" and couldn't slow down. Scientists speculate that the high use of bottled water in America and Canada explains why countries like India and China with low use of bottled water have significantly lower rates of ADHD.

The EPA reports, "studies in laboratory animals suggest that fetuses exposed to phthalates, chemicals used in plastics, can have multiple health issues as adults, including infertility, issues with genitalia development and sperm production problems. Also there are epidemiological studies showing developmental changes in children including late puberty in boys and early puberty in girls compared to previous generations."[56]

CBS news reports that BPA is widely found in consumer packaging, and it is used to line aluminum cans to protect them from corrosion. The chemical is also found in plastics such as bottles, Tupperware, tableware and food storage containers. The FDA has banned the use of BPA in baby bottles and "sippy cups" as of July 2012 due to concerns that the chemical could interfere with children's development.

> **FDA banned plastic body bottles with BPH**
> **due to concerns that the chemical**
> **could interfere with children's development.**

Due to a growing public awareness of the dangers of plastic many company's claim their plastic is "BPA free." Unfortunately, they simply replaced BPA with other kinds of plastic. Scientists at Georgetown University and the University of Texas claim these new BPA-free plastics are even worse, releasing chemicals with more estrogenic activity than the old BPA-containing products.[57]

13. Gluten Intolerance and other Food Sensitivities: One third of Americans are so compromised in the gut that they cannot tolerate gluten.[58] Gluten is particularly high in bread. Although wheat is not yet genetically modified, the fast-rising yeast used to make bread is genetically modified. This fast-rising yeast causes bread to have higher gluten levels, making it harder to digest. This indigestion then causes inflammation in the brain. By giving up gluten products, many people have reduced or eliminated ADHD symptoms.[59]

A multitude of studies have shown that, for many adults and children, food sensitivities are a major cause of ADHD. [60] Common culprits that can cause food allergies are gluten, non-fermented soy products (soy milk and tofu), "pasteurized" dairy products, GMO foods, corn, high fructose corn syrup, sugar, eggs, food dyes, preservatives, antibiotics, and/or artificial sweeteners. Food allergies and sensitivities cause gut inflammation, which in turn leads to inflammation in the brain and ADHD.

Food sensitivities cause gut inflammation, which in turn leads to inflammation in the brain and ADHD.

A double-blind study published in The Lancet gauged diet's effect on ADHD symptoms. Researchers recruited 100 children with ADHD, and placed 50 of them on a restricted diet, consisting mainly of rice, meat, vegetables, pears, and water, with some children getting a few other foods. The other 50, the control group, received their normal diet. At the end of five weeks, 64 percent of the children on the restricted diet had significant improvement in their ADHD symptoms, while none of the control group had improvements.[61]

14. Toxicity: Increasing levels of toxicity in the air we breath, the water we drink and the food we eat not only causes oxidative stress in the brain but it depletes the body of glutathione which can protect and heal the brain. The impact of this environmental stress on our body along with any of the factors listed above contributes to the oxidative stress in the brain that gives rise to ADHD.[62]

Neurotoxins are substances that injure the brain. They interact with nerve cells by over-stimulating them to death or interrupting their communication process. Neurotoxins are particularly dangerous when we don't have enough glutathione or minerals to protect the brain. This explains why some people are more influenced by them.

Neurotoxins are included in nearly all processed and packaged foods. The most common are:

1. Artificial sweeteners like aspartame and sucralose.

2. MSG or anything that has been hydrolyzed.

3. Soy protein (fermented soy is ok).

4. Aluminum (common in drinking water, over-the-counter antacids and vaccines.)

5. Mercury, which is common in fish products, silver fillings and vaccines. Mercury inhibits brain performance and is consistently linked to ADHD and the many symptoms of ASD (Autism Spectrum Disorder). Mercury blocks receptors sites in the brain from utilizing zinc, which in turn inhibits most brain functions. It is probably the most dangerous of all neurotoxins.

6. Fluoride, which is commonly added to our water supply. Read the warning labels on fluoridated toothpaste. They say, "Do not swallow" because fluoride is a known toxin. If we should not swallow it, then why are we adding it to our water supply?

Fluoride directly causes oxidative stress and displaces iodine, which is needed to neutralize oxidative stress. Pregnant mothers with iodine deficiencies have a 400% higher risk of having an autistic child. There is no good reason to put fluoride in our water. Even if putting fluoride in our water system helps decrease cavities in our children, there are others ways to minimize cavities without toxic side effects.

Everyday more cities and counties in America are opting out of adding fluoride to the water supply and rates of cavities have not increased. Go to Cleanwaterportland.org to learn more about the many reasons the citizens successfully stopped city officials from their repeated plans to add fluoride to the public drinking water.

There are other reasons we have low iodine levels. In 1980, the same year autism and ADHD levels began to soar; the American government mandated that commercial bread manufacturers stop using iodine in making bread dough. At the time there was a widespread fear of getting too much iodine. Today there is a new awareness that we need more iodine: breadmakers have now been mandated to use iodized salt.

In 1980, to replaced iodine, potassium bromate was used to condition flour. After ten years of use, potassium bromate was then discovered to be highly toxic. In the ninety's it was banned in Europe and the United Kingdom and in the 2000's it has been banned in China, Brazil and Peru. This banned toxic chemical, potassium bromate, has not been banned in America. In California a warning label is required on breads that have flour conditioned by potassium bromate.

This one change of replacing iodine with potassium bromate in our bread helps us to understand why so many people today cannot tolerate or digest the gluten in bread. Almost all children with ADHD experience immediate benefits from taking bread out of their diet.

To make matters even worse, bromate is like fluoride: it is not only toxic but it prevents the body from absorbing iodine. Both the use of fluoride in our water and bromine in our bread are major contributors to the ADHD and ASD epidemic. According to the CDC, states that have the highest use of fluoridated water have the highest rates of children diagnosed with rates of ADHD.

With a greater public awareness of the toxicity of potassium bromate, many breadmakers are finding new options. Traditional bread-making systems require a lengthy fermentation process to develop the dough. Modern systems are now moving on from using potassium bromate to using faster rising agents, which are made from toxic

GMOs. The manufacturers of these toxic breads are not mandated to disclose that they use GMOs in the fermentation process.

7. Pasteurized whey and casein dairy proteins (not to be confused with undenatured whey and casein proteins.) They are most common in children's baby formulas and energy bars.

8. Yeast extract, which is commonly found in canned foods.

9. EMFs and Wi-Fi pollution. Although electromagnetic frequencies (EMFs) are not in our food, they are in the air. EMFs from high power towers near schools have proven to increase a child's risk of cancer. No one disputes this fact. Yet, our exposure to EMFs continues to grow.

The use of smart phones dramatically increases our exposure to EMFs. I personally have seen its deadly effects. My niece developed terminal brain cancer because she was a big user of smart phones. Ann Louise Gittleman, a bestselling author on health and healing, was diagnosed with a tumor near her ear in 2005. In her book, Zapped, she reports studies that show increased oxidative stress from holding a cell phone for more than two hours on one side of the head, which she commonly did. In her book, she explores strategies for avoiding and navigating the damaging effects of electro-pollution. Keeping your cell phone away from your head by using the speaker mode and turning off your Wi-Fi at night can make a big difference. Various sources report that brain cancer is on the rise particularly in children who are more vulnerable to EMF's.

Recently, while cell phone companies dismiss any possible harm from EMFs, their smart phone instructions have changed to suggest not holding the phone closer than 5/8 of an inch to your head and body. In addition, they recommend keeping the smart phone away from the body and only use carrying cases, belt clips or holders that do not have metal parts and that maintain at least 5/8 of an inch separation between the phone and the body.

The main culprits of EMF pollution are not just smart phones. They include laptop computers, energy-efficient compact fluorescent lighting, cordless phones, Wi-Fi networks and smart phones. Short-term uses of these sources of EMF pollution are not a problem, it is the long-term exposure: how much and how long. The recent addition of "Smart Meters" is a new a major cause of oxidative stress. *Take Back Your Power* is an online movie that reveals this new alarming threat in greater detail with interviews with over 25 experts.

Everyday we are being bombarded with these neurotoxins. Our brain's health is dependent on our body's ability to neutralize the harmful effects of these neurotoxins as well cleanse them from the body. Children, however, are more vulnerable to these neurotoxins because their brains are still developing.[63]

**Children are more vulnerable to neurotoxins
because their brains are still developing.**

In addition to common neurotoxins, scientists have identified 201 common industrial chemicals as likely culprits contributing to ADHD and other mental disorders. "The bottom line is you only get one chance to develop a brain," said Philippe Grandjean, M.D., lead author of the study. "We have to protect children against chemical pollution because damage to a developing brain is irreversible."[64]

Studies from Columbia Center for Children's Environmental Health in New York City show that the air we breathe, which is filled with ambient toxins spewed by vehicles, pesticides in our food and chemicals found in common household products are all immediately detectable in the blood stream. Their research suggests that Moms are passing on these toxic chemicals to their babies. These toxins match what scientists are finding in the umbilical cord of their babies once they are born.[65]

The air we breathe, which is filled with ambient toxins spewed by vehicles, pesticides and chemicals.

These reports however do not take into consideration how adept a mother is at neutralizing the effects of toxicity by cleansing her body before pregnancy or stabilizing healthy levels of glutathione during her pregnancy. For example, women who take Tylenol, which suppresses glutathione, have a much higher risk of giving birth to children with ADHD, behavior problems, poor language and motor skills and communication difficulties.[66]

Women who take Tylenol,
have a much higher risk
of giving birth to children with ADHD.

Environmental toxins are attacking us every day. Our main hope in protecting ourselves is to minimize exposure while also helping the body detoxify. Detoxification requires occasional fasting and special supplements to sustain healthy glutathione levels. Mothers should not fast during pregnancy.

15. Nutritional Deficiencies: Over the past 100 years, farming practices using synthetic fertilizers have depleted the soil of the vitamins and minerals necessary to stimulate the production of brain chemicals. For example, when comparing the mineral content of food sixty years ago there has been an 80% drop in calcium and iron. When comparing the vitamin content most foods have had a drop of 75% in vitamin A and 50% in vitamin C.[67]

This common deficiency of minerals and vitamins means you must eat more food to get the nutrition you would have received in the past. You would have to eat four oranges today to get the same content of Vitamin A as our grandparents would have gotten from one. Foods that are genetically modified (GMOs) are even worse. One published study concluded that non-GMO corn compared to GMO corn is twenty times richer in nutrition.[68] These missing vitamins and minerals are all needed to protect the brain from oxidative stress.

Non-GMO corn compared to GMO corn
is twenty times richer in nutrition.

Iodine deficiency is also linked to oxidative stress. The World Health Organizations reports that iodine deficiency is one of the main causes of impaired cognitive development in children.[69] The common use of chlorine in our water, bromate in our bread yeast and fluoride in our water gradually depletes iodine in the body. According to the U.S. National Research Council "several lines of information indicate an effect of fluoride exposure on thyroid function."[70] Iodine is used by the thyroid gland not only to stimulate the metabolism but to detoxify the blood and protect the brain from oxidative stress. For more information about iodine go to MarsVenus.com/iodine.

Identify the Cause
to Recharge Your Brainpower

Oxidative stress is the one cause of ADHD but as we can see from the list above, there are many direct or indirect causes of oxidative stress. This expanded understanding of the many causes of oxidative stress gives us the necessary insight to heal ADHD.

By first eliminating the cause of oxidative stress and then providing the necessary support, the brain can heal itself. Even if you had a magic pill to heal oxidative stress, it wouldn't be much help if you keep causing more oxidative stress. The truth is your brain is designed to heal itself but only if we get out of the way and provide a little extra support.

With the right support,
the brain is designed to heal itself.

Each of these fifteen causes of chronic oxidative stress actually deplete your brain of the extra antioxidants necessary to not only protect brain cells but to recharge your brainpower. As explained before, antioxidants neutralize free radicals. Oxidative stress occurs when brain cells (neurons) are exposed to extra "free radicals" and your body is unable to neutralize these extra free radicals with antioxidants.

Antioxidants neutralize
free radicals to recharge your brain.

This oxidative stress not only injures brain cells but it also creates a condition that promotes the massive duplication of harmful pathogens (germs, bacteria, viruses, parasites and fungus). This is called an infection. In response to infection, the immune system attacks these germs by releasing free radicals. These free radicals produced by your immune system are targeted to kill the pathogens causing the infection. In this natural process, extra free radicals are produced. These extra free radicals become a new problem if the body cannot neutralize them.

The body is normally designed to produce extra antioxidants to "mop up" or neutralize these extra free radicals. But today, due to the influence of prescribed drugs, pesticides, toxicity and junk food, your body is unable to make the necessary amount of antioxidants to neutralize or mop up these extra free radicals.

These extra free radicals produced by our immune system in turn cause more oxidative stress in the brain. This ongoing oxidative stress causes chronic inflammation in the brain, which results in ADHD and a variety of other mental conditions. Natural solutions restore balance in the brain by decreasing exposure to free radicals and increasing production of antioxidants.

Natural solutions restore the
balance of free radicals and antioxidants.

A healthy body is designed to make free radicals to neutralize infection as well as the necessary antioxidants to neutralize them. In our modern world, we have an excess of free radicals and a deficiency of antioxidants. In the past, a simple concussion would heal all by itself. But today, with the high exposure to free radicals depleting our antioxidants, the natural healing of the brain is halted, whether it is from a concussion or oxidative stress caused by toxicity.

In some ways, the brain is like a battery. For a battery to produce energy, it requires both a positive charge and a negative charge. Without this balance, a battery will eventually lose its charge. In the brain, free radicals hold a positive charge and antioxidants hold a negative charge. When there are more free radicals (positive charge) than antioxidants (negative charge) the brain is drained of its energy. By restoring balance, the brain can be recharged and it can then heal itself.

The brain is like a battery which
can be recharged.

By reducing your exposure to toxicity and increasing your production of antioxidants natural solutions can and will recharge your brain just like recharging a battery.

The body is designed to recharge the brain by producing both free radicals and antioxidants. Beneficial free radicals are naturally produced by exercising and challenging your body and mind while antioxidants are produced by authentic emotions and positive feelings fueled by healthy mineral-rich nutritious food.

Chapter Five

Does ADHD Ever Go Away?

In the past, many people believed symptoms of ADHD commonly go away as we move out of childhood and into adulthood. I have observed the opposite in my clients. In childhood, ADHD shows up in more obvious ways, but as our brains continue to develop and our coping skills increase, the condition causing ADHD in childhood continues on, often unacknowledged but inhibiting our potential for personal fulfillment.

While growing up, our brains continue to develop, but unless the original oxidative stress is healed, the brain develops in a way to compensate for oxidative stress rather than according to its normal design.

The ADHD brain compensates for oxidative stress rather than develop according to its normal design.

Understanding brain science can be quite complex, but this same concept can be easily understood if we apply it to a broken bone that needs to be healed.

If you have a broken bone in childhood, the bone will automatically grow back because the body is designed to heal itself. But unless the bone is properly "reset," according to the body's design, it will not grow back straight. By resetting the bone, and providing extra protection from further injury with a cast, it not only grows back, it actually ends up stronger than it was before the break.

In a similar way, by recognizing the oxidative stress that causes ADHD and then "resetting" the brain with extra support, while also providing protection from future oxidative stress, the brain can grow back according to its natural healthy design. It may even grow back stronger. The extra support necessary to "reset" the brain can be a combination of physical, emotional, mental, sensory, and nutritional support. We will explore these different modes of support later in Appendix Four.

By "resetting" the brain, we can heal ADHD.

To begin the process of healing we must first recognize the symptoms of ADHD. By identifying the many faces and later stages of ADHD we can then address the cause and eventually heal the condition. Without first recognizing that we have ADHD, we are not motivated to seek out and find the answers to heal our condition.

To make matters worse, without the recognition that ADHD is a physical condition of oxidative stress in the brain, we tend to be become overly critical of others or ourselves. We continue to misinterpret ADHD symptoms as character defects, neurosis and/or personal failings.

With this new insight we can view the symptoms of ADHD in others and ourselves in a more compassionate light. We can react to ADHD as we would react to having a broken leg and needing to walk with crutches for a few months.

ADHD does not have to be a lifelong sentence. It can be healed. For some, this insight means they don't have to take dangerous drugs to medicate the condition. For others, it means they become less defensive about having a "disorder" or "mental condition." They are then free to focus on getting the extra nutrition their brain requires. With this new insight the door opens to explore natural solutions to heal ADHD.

The Many Stages of ADHD

Throughout life our brain continues to grow and develop. Complex brain changes continue into old age, which reflect our degrees of maturity. At every stage of life, ADHD interferes with our normal development and the expression of our inner potential for success, happiness, love and good health.

Let's take a brief overview of the new challenges caused by ADHD at six major stages of brain development and maturity:

Stage 1. Children experience different degrees of trauma related to learning, behavior and social challenges. The inability to excel in the classroom or form supportive friendships can seriously limit one's happiness, self-image and self-esteem along with his or her ability to trust.

Stage 2. Teens experience new social challenges including isolation, bullying, body image, obesity and addictions. While violence and video addiction is increasing in boys, girls are experiencing more body image problems and bullying. Boys experience late puberty and girls experience early puberty.

Stage 3. Young adults experience increasing degrees of depression and anxiety and commonly return home after college to live with their parents. More young men and women are unwilling to make lasting commitments in intimate relationships. Divorce continues to be high, shorter relationships are the norm and there are now twice as many single people.

Stage 4. Adults experience an increasing inability to manage stress levels, which in turn leads to dissatisfaction in relationships, overwhelm, exhaustion and divorce.

Stage 5. At midlife, aging adults face some version of the "midlife crisis" which includes boredom in relationships, depression based on regret, and/or boredom with work and a longing to quit and retire.

Stage 6. Elders today experience unprecedented levels of modern diseases that were previously not common including diabetes, heart disease, cancer, Parkinson's disease, dementia and Alzheimer's disease.

All of these challenges arise from the same condition that gives rise to ADHD but go unrecognized as such.

The Unrecognized Symptoms of ADHD

As we age, our brain continues to grow and develop through different stages. At each stage, if ADHD is not healed it continues on in new and different ways. The childhood symptoms shift into teenage symptoms and so on. The symptoms of each stage remain to some degree but are overlooked or suppressed as new coping mechanisms emerge.

A coping mechanism is not always a good thing. For example, a young ADHD child may inappropriately express painful emotions. As they become older a coping mechanism may simply be the repression of their ability to feel emotions.

They no longer inappropriately feel and express painful emotions but they are also unable to feel and express their positive emotions as well. When asked what they feel, they feel nothing, while layers of repressed feelings and limiting beliefs are hidden deep inside their hearts.

**A coping mechanism
is not necessarily a good thing.**

Lets explore common coping mechanisms of ADHD that may emerge according to the four temperaments.

1. Coping mechanisms for creative children: At puberty, children with a creative temperament who are hyper-focused on seeking new stimulation may no longer be spaced out, bored or distracted in the classroom. Instead, they learn to cope by creating a kind of tunnel vision or focus that allows them to excel at one thing but limits their ability to enjoy other interests. With great enthusiasm, they may start new projects but quickly lose interest, procrastinate or simply do not follow through. They may create unnecessary drama by waiting to the last minute to finish tasks.

**They start new projects but quickly
lose interest, procrastinate or
simply do not follow through.**

As adults in relationships, they can be hyper-focused on loving their partner in the beginning but may just as quickly lose interest, moving on to a new partner or a new focus that provides a new challenge. They tend to be hot and cold in their relationships. They do not realize that their lack of commitment in a relationship is a symptom of ADHD, but feel they have just lost that loving feeling and have no idea why.

2. Coping mechanisms for responsible children: A child at puberty with a responsible temperament who is hyper-controlling may stop resisting change but as a teenager they may become obsessed with being perfect. They may become high achievers but never feel good enough. They may also become overly stubborn, rebellious or defiant.

On the other hand, they may compensate by becoming obedient to the wishes of others or their parents. They may become excessively vulnerable to peer pressure. As adults they may climb the ladder of success and eventually discover they were climbing up the wrong wall.

> **They may climb the ladder of success**
> **and eventually discover**
> **they were climbing up the wrong wall.**

In relationships, they are often disappointed and may feel they give more and get less. They are often rejected or criticized for being too judgmental or too controlling. They do not recognize that their need for perfection is excessive and a symptom of ADHD. They feel misunderstood because they are only trying to make things better.

In some cases, they may cope with these symptoms of ADHD by overeating, over-exercising or oversleeping. They mistakenly conclude they just like to overeat, oversleep or over-exercise.

3. Coping mechanisms for bold children: When children with a bold temperament who are hyperactive become teenagers, they may be able to sit still in class but their minds remain busy, distracted or bored. They may stop fidgeting but in their minds they are somewhere else. It is hard for them to stay focused on a particular train of thought.

Hyperactive teens or adults may develop the coping mechanism of becoming thrill seekers to avoid feeling bored with the routine of life. Rather than consider their "dangerous thrill seeking" as a coping mechanism for ADHD to suppress the feelings of boredom, they conclude, "I just like to do dangerous things."

**They become thrill seekers to
avoid feeling bored with the routine of life.**

They may be unable to relax and enjoy the moment and mistakenly assume that is just the way they are. They are always busy moving towards some future goal but unable to appreciate what they have in the moment. Their minds keep them constantly busy thinking up new things to either worry about or achieve.

4. Coping mechanisms for sensitive children: Children with a sensitive temperament who are hyper-vulnerable may develop the coping mechanism of repressing their need for love and as a result resist or reject affection, appreciation or intimacy.

They may become hardened by life and relationships and become overly self-reliant and independent. They always wear a smile because they are determined to not get hurt by depending on another. They can be very loving and giving but are not good at receiving. In intimate relationships, they are easily disappointed and may become moody, anxious or depressed.

**They become hardened by life
and become overly self-reliant and independent.**

As adults, they may become overly caring for others to avoid feeling their own vulnerable feelings. Eventually the denial of their own needs catches up and they feel alone, resentful or hurt. Rather than recognizing over-giving as a symptom of ADHD, they may just blame others for not supporting or appreciating them enough.

Understanding Coping Mechanisms

Understanding coping mechanisms helps us to question and discover who we truly are. Are we simply coping with an abnormal brain condition or are we expressing our true and authentic self? Coping mechanisms can be so automatic that we just assume they express who we are instead of recognizing that we may have ADHD.

In these examples, coping mechanisms are automatic reactions, attitudes or behaviors to avoid feeling the original symptoms of our ADHD. They often feel good because they help us to avoid the discomfort of having symptoms of ADHD.

**Coping mechanisms help us avoid
the discomfort of having symptoms of ADHD.**

For example, if procrastination to achieve a goal is uncomfortable, a coping mechanism may be oversleeping or making something else more important and doing that. One may even decide to stay in their comfort zone by giving up their goal altogether.

When ADHD is not recognized, we can easily delude ourselves and become addicted to our coping mechanisms. Even actual drug addictions are coping mechanisms to minimize the symptoms of ADHD. Drug addicts medicate their ADHD with drugs. They may say, " I am not addicted to pot, I just like to do it. Otherwise life is too boring. I just do it for fun." This is commonly called "denial."

With the automatic development of coping mechanisms when ADHD is not healed, we gradually disconnect from our ability to know our true feelings. We lose focus on what is most important in life and as a result we give importance to what is not really important.

For example, money becomes more important than love. Pleasure becomes more important than our health. The approval of others becomes more important than being true to ourselves. Looking good becomes more important than honesty or integrity. With ADHD, we lose our way; we forget why we are here. For many, life loses a sense of meaning and purpose.

This is a list of common coping mechanism to self-medicate the symptoms of ADHD:

1. Addiction to pornography, excessive masturbation and all substance abuse.

2. Increase in short-term relationships and an inability to commit to long-term loving relationships. Couples are still living together and getting married but many more are not getting married. 58% of first births in lower-middle-class households are now to unmarried women. Meanwhile, two out of five births are to unwed mothers. When the Wall Street Journal asks the question "Why so many babies?" a better question would be "Why so few marriages?"[1]

3. Dramatic increase in men and women who stay single and don't get married. The number of single adults has increased one hundred percent in the last sixty years. Married couples have dropped to below half of all American households. Compared to 1950 there are now twice as many single adults.[2]

4. Dramatic increase in obesity due to increased consumption of processed junk foods and sugar products, which affect the brain in the same way as stimulant drugs. More than two-thirds of adult Americans are overweight, half of them are considered obese. One out of six children are considered obese and the numbers are increasing every year.[3]

5. Dramatic increase in caffeine consumption. Besides seeing a Starbucks on every corner, super-caffeinated drinks like Rock Star, Mountain Dew, Red Bull and 5-Hour Energy dominate the energy drink industry. Caffeine mimics the same pathways as stimulant drugs. Two shots of espresso provide the same stimulation as one small dose of Ritalin. Teens and adults may stop their Ritalin

but it is being replaced with caffeine addiction. The number one complaint doctors hear from patients is increased tiredness and fatigue.[4] Excessive caffeine consumption leads to chronic fatigue, which in turn leads to increased caffeine consumption. An exhausting cycle.

6. The massive use of erectile dysfunction drugs like Viagra and Cialis to sustain an erection in a committed relationship.[5] It is estimated that one out of five men over 45 have used these drugs.[6] Many men are unable to be turned on to their long-term partner but can easily get turned on to porn or a new relationship. The downregulation of dopamine receptors in ADHD causes millions of adults to lose interest in their partners. When their partners are no longer new or novel, their interest and attraction fades away.

7. Men become overly engaged in their work and lose focus on their partners. The number one complaint married women have about their husbands is, "he doesn't listen."

8. Women become overly focused on the needs of others and become overwhelmed feeling frustrated that there is no time for them.

9. While addiction to video games is a teenage symptom of ADHD, adults are commonly addicted to work, sports, movies or TV. More men and women complain today that the passion in their relationships or for their work has faded away. This symptom mimics the same symptoms as an ADHD child who quickly loses focus and interest in his schoolwork.

10. Massive numbers of people are addicted to a sedentary lifestyle sitting in front of a computer or TV to avoid feeling the boredom of ADHD. Others cope with boredom by an addiction to excessive exercise to the point of injury.

Recognizing how we avoid the pain, boredom, lack of focus and procrastination associated with ADHD, frees us to begin the journey of true self-discovery, authentic self-reflection and the expression of our inner genius potential.

CHAPTER SIX

How Stimulant Drugs Change Your Child's Brain

Recent brain scans reveal a distinction in brain activity associated with ADHD that can last a lifetime.[1] This research implies that without natural solutions to heal the brain, the various challenges associated with ADHD do not disappear with age. Even stimulant drugs used to treat ADHD, like Ritalin or Adderall, do not, nor do they claim to, heal the condition. They affect the brain in the same way as any other addictive drug or addictive behavior. One of the main differences between Ritalin and cocaine is that the doses of stimulant drugs for children are smaller than what you would take as a drug addict.[2]

At best, stimulant drugs temporarily mask the symptoms of ADHD until the condition shows up in different ways. The use of stimulant drugs may minimize symptoms of ADHD in the beginning, but over time oxidative stress in the brain actually becomes worse than if you had done nothing. A good analogy to understand the long-term effect of stimulant drugs is the continued use of drugs to treat Parkinson's disease.

L-dopa, which is similar to a stimulant drug, helps to alleviate symptoms of Parkinson's disease but over time you have to take more and more until it finally stops working and nothing will help. The more you take it, the less effective it becomes.

The more drugs you take, the less effective they are.

To control symptoms, you have to gradually take bigger doses until the drug stops working. The reason it stops working is that with each use, the original brain condition of oxidative stress that caused the symptoms of Parkinson's disease gets worse and worse. While taking the drug, symptoms temporarily go away but the condition actually gets worse.

Why Drugs Do Not Heal

With a deeper understanding about stimulant drugs, it becomes clear why stimulants should only be used as a last resort or for a temporary time period. Stimulants produce high amounts of dopamine, the brain chemical of focus, pleasure, interest and motivation. This sounds great except that overstimulation by high amounts of dopamine changes the brain.

With repeated high stimulation from drug-induced dopamine function, other normal levels of stimulation like learning in class or listening to your parents no longer have the power to grip your attention. Unless you are being over stimulated, life becomes boring, less fun, less interesting and you lose your natural motivations.

With repeated drug use,
life becomes boring and flat.

This is why people become addicted to drugs. Without the overstimulation provided by the continued use of the drug, life is not worth living.

In lay language, after repeated use of an addictive drug one develops "tolerance." This means that over time the brain has significantly changed and only a higher dose can have the same effect. It also means normal stimulation is no longer fulfilling.

**"Tolerance" due to drugs means the brain has changed
and only a higher dose can have an effect.**

This dynamic applies to all addictions. In the beginning, only a little sugar is needed to feel good, but later you need more. In the beginning, only an hour of playing a video game is needed but after a while the brain hungers for more. In the beginning, it only takes one drink to forget your problems, but after a few drinks, if you have the gene that converts alcohol to dopamine, then your brain wants more. In the beginning, a little cocaine is needed to get high, but after a while the brain hungers for more. With every addiction, as tolerance sets in, we gradually lose our ability to respond to life's normal experiences with sustained focus, pleasure, interest or motivation.

Dopamine and Your Brain

In scientific terms, the overstimulation by alcohol, video games, high amounts of sugar or stimulant drugs increases the release of dopamine and with this overstimulation dopamine receptor sites in the brain "downregulate." The downregulation of dopamine receptor sites means the number of dopamine receptors on each brain neuron temporarily decrease in number.

**Drugs take you up
but there is always a down.**

When the dopamine receptors return and increase in number, it is called the upregulation of dopamine receptors. With upregulated receptor sites we are no longer dependent on overstimulation for focus, pleasure, interest and motivation; normal stimulation is enough and addictive tendencies decrease.

The Two Keys for Understanding ADHD

Understanding these new terms "dopamine" and "downregulation" is crucial for every parent. Although these terms are not part of our normal conversation, it is important for your child's health and happiness to become very familiar with them. These two concepts hold the key to understanding and healing ADHD.

1. Dopamine: The brain chemical dopamine is associated with focus, motivation, interest and pleasure. Inhibited dopamine function creates the symptoms of ADHD in four unique and sometimes opposite ways:

1. Decreased focus gives rise to increased distraction, a resistance to finishing things and hyper-pleasure from new experiences or sharing something new with others. These symptoms of ADHD are associated with the creative temperament and often diagnosed as ADHD distracted.
2. Decreased motivation gives rise to an increased sedentary lifestyle, resistance to change or new experiences and hyper-focus on details, routine and control. This symptom of ADHD is associated with the responsible temperament and is often diagnosed as obsessive-compulsive disorder.
3. Decreased interest gives rise to increased boredom, resistance to routine or sedentary lifestyle, and hyper-motivation for self-expression through action, movement or speech. This is associated with the bold temperament and is often diagnosed as ADHD impulsive.
4. Decreased pleasure gives rise to increased physical or emotional pain or sensitivity, a resistance to intense stimulation or confrontation and hyper-interest in what they feel and in what others think. This is associated with the

sensitive temperament and is often diagnosed as having a mood disorder.

2. Downregulation of Receptor Sites: Dopamine receptor sites downregulate with overstimulation. In the absence of overstimulation, receptor sites return to normal by upregulation. Drugs downregulate receptor sites creating the need for more drugs, while healing the brain up-regulates brain receptor sites.

Chapter Seven

The Key to Healing The Brain

Understanding dopamine receptors is the key to healing the brain. These brain receptors are designed to automatically upregulate, but only if the overstimulation stops. Being fully relaxed and rested helps the receptors upregulate and return to normal. Brain injuries, oxidative stress or continued use of stimulant drugs prevent the automatic upregulation of brain receptor sites.

For example, if you have an exciting evening, lots of dopamine gets produced which downregulates your dopamine receptors. As a result, the next morning you may feel a little flat or bored. But after a few hours your dopamine receptors upregulate and you are back to feeling normal.

But if you drank too much or had too much sugar, the increased degree of oxidative stress delays the upregulation of dopamine receptors and you have a hangover.

When a child or adult takes an ADHD stimulant drug, more dopamine is released and downregulation of dopamine receptor sites gradually occurs. As the number of receptor sites on each brain neuron decrease, more stimulation is required to experience focus, pleasure, interest or motivation. When the effects of the drug wear off, the symptoms of ADHD return.

**When the effects of stimulant drugs
wear off, the symptoms of ADHD return.**

To restore focus, pleasure, interest and motivation and avoid the discomfort or boredom of inhibited dopamine function, the brain craves more of the drug or other addictive activities. This increased stimulation releases more dopamine.

In practical terms, when receptors downregulate, normal levels of stimulation from the world and relationships have less effect. Instead of being interested in what the teacher or parent says, the child is bored, restless or distracted. With downregulated receptors, the normal stimulation that comes from wanting to make Mom and Dad happy or proud has less effect on the child's brain.

**For some children with ADHD,
the natural desire for parental approval
has less effect on the child's brain.**

A child with upregulated receptor sites is primarily motivated by a deep desire to please their parents to insure getting their love and support. But with ADHD, the automatic pleasure and motivation to please one's parent is simply background noise compared to the loud demands of addictive stimulants and behaviors. The fundamental internal programming to please their parents, which motivates children to listen, behave and cooperate, becomes less important. It is replaced by a new drive to seek out excessive stimulation.

**A child with upregulated receptors is
automatically motivated
by a deep desire to please their parents.**

With downregulated receptors, foods with high sugar content and addictive behaviors like video games that stimulate the brain to make more dopamine become more dominant motivators and sources of greater pleasure. In short, the ADHD brain or the brain after taking ADHD drugs is saying, "I want to make my parents happy but I want to play this game or eat this junk food more."

> **The ADHD child's brain is saying,**
> **"I want to please my parents but**
> **I want to play video games more."**

In the beginning of ADHD stimulant drug use, with plenty of dopamine being released the child will be more attentive and interested in what parents have to say and with their schoolwork. But after continued use, as dopamine receptors downregulate and "tolerance" sets in, the child's brain once again becomes more easily distracted, bored, impulsive, stressed, uninterested or simply unmotivated. Long-term studies have confirmed that on average after using stimulant drugs ADHD symptoms return within three years.[1]

Some parents reason, "At least in the short run my child can be successful in school with his studies and social interactions."

While this is true sometimes, the risks of common side effects like stunted growth, weight loss and long-term brain changes must also be considered.[2] To this a parent might counter, "Yes, but having three years of a happy childhood and education could at least prepare my child to overcome their ADHD tendencies later in life." This argument certainly has merit.

But, this whole discussion becomes irrelevant when non-drug solutions are available. The question is not, "Do we use drugs or not?" but instead it becomes "Which nutritional supplements are best for my child?"

**By using drugs for ADHD, we have
called off the search for a lasting solution.**

Taking ADHD drugs to temporarily mask the symptoms of oxidative stress does nothing to change the conditions that derail a child's development in the first place. By focusing on drugs as a solution to the ADHD epidemic, the medical community has called off the search for a comprehensive understanding of the condition.

CHAPTER EIGHT

The Long-Term Side Effects of Stimulant Drugs

With this new insight into the long-term side effects of using stimulant drugs, parents can no longer consider drug use in a casual manner. Taking stimulant drugs for ADHD, just like other addictive substances, makes a child need the drug more and their parents less. Stimulants not only increase "tolerance" to the drug but to all external stimulation. By providing stimulant drugs, we are setting up our children for a lifetime of addictive cravings for substances and behaviors to self-medicate their ADHD.

> **By providing stimulant drugs,
> we are setting up our children
> for a lifetime of addictive cravings.**

When most kids stop their stimulant medications as teenagers, they often move into other legal or illegal addictions to medicate themselves. Besides increasing addiction, this crisis also affects our children's ability to form loving and lasting relationships. With ADHD, a growing number of men are less motivated to make a commitment in relationships while more women are focusing on their careers and waiting longer to get married.

The rising tide of ADHD has disturbed the historic balance of men and women creating a new inequality. Twice as many boys are diagnosed with ADHD[1] and over sixty percent of college graduates are girls and not boys.[2] That means two girls for every boy. This imbalance is directly increasing the number of unmarried men and women. As mentioned before, there are now twice as many single men and women.

**Twice as many boys are diagnosed with ADHD
and over sixty percent of college graduates are girls.**

Most female college graduates and non-graduates who are interested in forming a loving relationship are looking for a man with a college degree. A college degree is certainly a symbol of one who has a greater earning potential. On popular dating sites, men who have a job and own a house experience a long list of women pursuing them.

With a shortage of men who have graduated, women are not only pursuing college graduates but competing with each other for men. It used to be men pursuing and competing with each other for the women. The whole dating scene has now turned upside down. With an abundance of women pursuing men, single men have become more passive and unwilling to commit. This shift confirms the somewhat offensive old adage, "Why buy the cow when you can get the milk for free?"

**With an abundance of women looking for men,
men have become more passive and unwilling to commit.**

It used to be that the motivation to please a girl or get a girlfriend influenced boys to behave better in all areas of life. But today with ADHD, boys don't care as much. With less hope for a better life, their behavior becomes disruptive. Two boys to every girl are

suspended or expelled from high school.[3] With more girls competing for the decreasing number of high performing males it creates
a hopelessness in other boys. As a result, four times as many males
commit suicide.[4] There are certainly other reasons for committing
suicide but ADHD inspired hopelessness sits at the top of the list.

While alcohol addiction is now less at college, the illegal use
of amphetamines along with Ritalin and Adderall is dramatically up. Even without the use of these drugs, the casual use of
Internet pornography, junk food, video games or highly-caffein-
ated drinks can easily supply the excessive stimulation they seek.
These addictive behaviors and substances temporarily relieve the
symptoms of ADHD but over time they continue to change the
brain and make the problem worse.

This problem of casual addiction to porn is not just in
America, it is global. Pornography has become so addictive and
pervasive that globally it is a $98 billion dollar a year industry
with 14% in America, 21% in Japan, 27% in South Korea and 29%
in China.[5] Online pornography is so pervasive that 12% of all
websites have to do with sex.[6]

**This problem of casual addiction to porn
is not just in America, it is global.**

The global sex industry makes billions of dollars every year.[7] At
the very least, giving your children ADHD drugs today is simply
making them vulnerable to the most common addictive substances
like sugar and caffeine and then addictive behaviors like video
games and Internet pornography.

On the other hand, when the brain is properly fed the nutrients to make healthy brain chemicals, the ADHD child will be
sufficiently stimulated and motivated by the opportunity to please
their parents and teachers. In time, as the brain heals, symptoms
of ADHD and addictive tendencies gradually disappear.

All children will still have their own challenges according to their unique temperament, but without ADHD they will not be "hyper" challenges. Healing ADHD does not mean that every child will have a perfect childhood or become a child prodigy, but it does mean they will have a normal childhood to develop their full potential and have the opportunity to express their inner genius.

CHAPTER NINE

Proven Solutions for Increasing Brain Performance

Although the media doesn't talk about them and your doctor probably doesn't know about them, there are an abundance of natural solutions for increasing brain performance. Researchers have discovered that different combinations of healthy exercise, better diets, detox protocols, extra nutritional support, body work, behavioral support and counseling are a better approach to improving brain performance. In Chapters Nine through Thirteen, we will explore these different solutions in greater detail.

In *Book Two*, we will explore various mental, emotional and behavioral strategies to lower stress and increase your happiness and success in life. The first step, however, is to provide the support necessary to reduce oxidative stress in the brain. This first step is the foundation of lasting positive change. A brief overview of these natural solutions will help you find what will work for you and your family.

A brief overview of natural solutions
will help you find what will work for you and your family.

These natural solutions do not cure disease but awaken and support the body and brain in restoring normal health. These valuable insights will insure clear thinking and stronger focus for you and your family. Even if you don't have ADHD, or don't know you have ADHD, you will gain many valuable insights for improving your brain performance.

Increased Exercise
Can Reverse Symptoms of ADHD

One of the most obvious contributing factors that cause ADHD in children is lack of exercise. The early stages of brain development are particularly dependent on physical exercise and bodily movement. Regular, challenging and varied physical movement is required to develop the brain's ability to sustain healthy and appropriate focus. Without it, many children with ADHD simply cannot focus in school and often don't listen to their parents at home.

Brain scans in children have revealed that the brain actually changes its structure in reaction to various stimulation or lack of stimulation. Challenging physical exercise and new movements of the body have proven to create the most dramatic and positive changes in brain development.[1] This ability of the brain to adapt and change is described as brain plasticity. The study of brain plasticity is an exciting new field of brain research.

Up until the last two decades, brain scientists thought the brain stopped developing after the first few years of life. They believed brain connections were formed in an early critical period and, if a particular area was injured due to oxidative stress, those nerve cells could not form new connections or regenerate. New research has overturned this mistaken old view. At all stages of life, the brain has the potential to regenerate and reorganize itself to compensate for oxidative stress.[2]

Dr. Anat Baniel explains, "the moment we pay attention to our movement, the brain resumes growing at a very rapid rate.[3] For example, research reveals significant changes occur in the brain when a person practices a new song on the piano. By repeating the hand movements for about two hours over a period of five days, significant brain growth occurred.[4] Brain scans have revealed that those kids who play musical instruments have significantly more grey matter volume in the brain.[5] This new research into brain plasticity confirms that physical movement is one of the most powerful brain stimulators for developing a child's brain.

Physical movement is a powerful brain stimulant that helps develop a child's brain.

Other research has demonstrated that with increased supervised exercise at school, grades go up and behavior dramatically improves. In the Urban Dove High School, school administrators collected the lowest performing students from other schools and helped them become high achieving students.[6]

They created a radically new and more supportive environment for the children. For the first three hours, the curriculum included different kinds of gender-specific, supervised physical exercise and competitive sports. The children were also mentored later in the day between academic classes by their gym coaches with whom they had formed a bond. The results were miraculous.

The outcome of this new curriculum was that ninety-eight percent of the children graduated from high school and ninety percent went on to college. Without this kind of intervention, not one of the children was expected to graduate from high school or attend college.

Without intervention, not one of the children was expected to attend college.

The success of this program does not mean that every child just needs more exercise, nor does it mean that the absence of exercise is the primary cause of ADHD. But it does show that our children, particularly those with learning challenges, have tremendous untapped potential. With a more holistic approach, combined with other non-drug solutions, a more moderate exercise program would be equally effective.

Art Class Improves Brain Function

Art therapy has shown to help students with ADHD reduce impulsive behaviors, enhance interpersonal behavior and improve study skills and classroom performance.[7] Reading, writing and math primarily require left-brain activity. For all children, using art to increase activity on the right side of the brain has shown to increase grades and improve behavior in children.[8]

Art has shown to increase grades and improve behavior in children.

By setting goals using the left brain and then using the right brain by drawing colored pictures of what achieving those goals would look like, dramatic and positive changes result in both children and adults. According to Brian Mayne, this process of "Goal Mapping" has assisted over 100,000 children to improve brain performance by activating the whole of their brain through the combined use of words and pictures.[9]

While writing my first book 30 years ago, *What You Feel You Can Heal*, due to my own ADHD, I would get stuck focusing on one idea and had difficulty flowing from one topic to another. As I mentioned before, one of my ADHD symptoms was hyperfocus. I overcame this tendency by writing for a page and then taking time to draw a cartoon summarizing the idea I was writing about. Drawing a picture required that I shift from my dominate left-brain activity to use my right brain. This shift allowed me to use my whole brain and develop my ability to express my ideas and write books.

Using art to increase activity on the right side of the brain improves grades and behavior.

Without this vital insight about brain development, unfortunately most schools in America have eliminated both gym class for exercise and art classes for right-brain stimulation. Instead, they focus primarily on left-brain activities like reading, writing and math. Providing both left and right-brain activities can stimulate whole brain development.

CHAPTER TEN

Natural Supplements Outperform Prescribed Drugs

With the help of a few natural solutions, sometimes oxidative stress in the brain can be healed in weeks. One of my friends, who is a very successful business coach, experienced "road rage." He had learned to control its expression, but he still had to endure it. It definitely limited his ability to relax and enjoy his success.

After getting brain scans at a popular brain clinic, he was told he had dramatic brain injuries and damage. He had played football in college and had experienced many concussions. They said his brain scan was one of the worst they had seen. He was prescribed a list of drugs to suppress the symptoms. He gave me a call for some alternative advice.

I merely suggested a few specific vitamin and mineral supplements that I list in Appendix One and the condition improved within weeks. When he returned to the brain clinic two months later, they were amazed by the positive changes in his brain as revealed by the brain scan. By using natural solutions that support brain healing, he eliminated the need to take any drugs.

In many cases, one of the most effective natural solutions for ADHD is a natural supplement called Pycnogenol. In a double-blind study, over a period of 4 weeks, 61 children with ADHD took 50 mgs a day of Pycnogenol. The results show a significant reduction of hyperactivity and improved concentration. In the placebo group no positive effects were found.[1]

**Pycnogenol reduced
ADHD symptoms in four weeks.**

Pycnogenol is the natural extract of pine bark. It has been used for over 60 years as an all-natural remedy for inflammation of the joints. It is a super antioxidant that helps heal inflammation in the joints and the brain as well. It contains Oligomeric Proanthocyanidins, also known as OPCs, which are super antioxidants known to reduce inflammation. A cheaper alternative to Pycnogenol that is also rich in OPCs is grape seed extract.

In another study, one group of children with ADHD were given stimulant drugs like Ritalin or Adderall and another group was given a combination of vitamin C and OPCs. The short-term benefits in both groups were the same except the natural supplement group had no side effects.[2] OPCs help to activate the antioxidant benefit of Vitamin C and Vitamin E by 50 times. When there is oxidative stress in the brain, antioxidants help to heal the brain.

**Vitamin C and grape seed extract
taken together can outperform drugs.**

Another school program showed dramatic results when students were educated about the importance of good diet and exercise. In addition, students took two chewable multivitamins every day. This was not an ordinary multivitamin. Just a few of its extra ingredients were higher doses of Vitamin K, Vitamin C and Vitamin D along with a unique blend of fruit and berry concentrates high in antioxidants like the OPCs listed above. In addition, it contained 500 mgs of the amino acid L-taurine, which is known to stabilize levels of dopamine. For more information about this amazing daily vitamin, visit **MarsVenus.com/potential**.

**Special multivitamins have proven
to improve brain performance.**

This school had been the lowest performing public school on the East Coast and within a year became one of the best. The results were so miraculous that PBS made a documentary of the success.[3] The program has continued on for the last 8 years.

These are some of the benefits reported in this turnaround program called, "Eat, Exercise, Excel."

- #1 in school district in Math
- #2 in school district for English
- 40 children met Presidential Physical Fitness Standards. Only three children met these standards the previous year
- 95% reduction in referrals for anti-social behavior
- 80% reduction in out-of-school suspensions
- 97% reduction in suspension for violence
- Teachers report less difficulty managing classroom
- 80% reduction in teacher attrition
- Reduced absenteeism for teachers & students
- Volunteers & community partnerships increased

In another case study, researchers confirmed that a monitored program of amino acid supplementation with over-the-counter supplements such as l-tyrosine, 5-HTP, l-cysteine and a multivitamin could stop the progression of Parkinson's disease without side effects and in some cases even reverse the condition.[4] A modified version of this program was found to completely reverse symptoms of ADHD suggesting that the efficacy of this treatment protocol to be potentially superior to results seen with prescription drugs.[5] Details of this program and other variations can be found at **MarsVenus.com/ADHD**.

**Amino acid supplements reverse
Parkinson's disease and ADHD.**

The most important distinction between these different natural solutions for ADHD and stimulant drugs is that these natural solutions have no side effects. They gradually heal the condition while drugs do not heal. In the long-term, drugs slowly make the condition worse. With all these studies, it is still surprising to me how many people do not believe in the power of supplements and choose to use drugs.

Sometimes, seeing is believing. You can visually witness the profound effects of natural supplementation for Parkinson's disease on YouTube. Just one intravenous treatment of glutathione can dramatically reduce the symptoms of progressed Parkinson's disease. For more information, watch Dr. David Perlmutter's "Parkinson's-Glutathione Therapy" video at http://www.youtube.com/watch?v=KWuOezgVHdI.

Omega-3 Support
Increases Cognitive Performance

In his bestselling book, *Grain Brain*, Dr. Perlmutter reveals his protocol for correcting symptoms of ADHD. He has experienced that with ADHD, positive results are quickly achieved by taking children off gluten products and giving them 300 mg a day of DHA omega-3. DHA omega-3 has also been shown to improve learning and memory, and support cognitive health with aging.[6]

Repeatedly, researchers find that children with ADHD have low levels of omega-3 fatty acids. While omega-3 oils can help, as many studies indicate, when combined with vitamin C, it is even more effective. A study in India demonstrated that supplementation with flax oil (rich in omega-3) and vitamin C provided significant improvement in children with ADHD.[7]

One of the challenges with flax oil is that it can easily go rancid. Both sprouted fax and chia are rich sources of omega-3 and they do not easily go rancid. These can easily be added to your morning shake. They are not only rich in omega-3 but also help to balance blood sugar and keep you regular.

An Australian study has shown that the use of omega-3 fish oils is more effective for treating ADHD than Ritalin and Concerta, the drugs most often prescribed for ADHD in Australia.[8]

**Omega-3 fish oil is more effective
for treating ADHD than Ritalin and Concerta.**

Some children with ADHD have not benefited from extra omega-3. Due to elevated stress levels, weight gain or high insulin levels, they are unable to metabolize beneficial omega-3 fats. To counteract this tendency, one or two grams daily of acetyl-l-carnitine can assist the body in utilizing the omega-3 supplements better.[9]

Phosphatidylserine
Improves Memory and Mood

Various research studies reveal that supplementation with the natural ingredient Phosphatidylserine (PS), commonly found in egg yolks, improves memory, mood and even reduces ADHD symptoms. In one study, 78 elderly people with mild cognitive impairment were given PS supplements, or a placebo. At the end of six months, participants taking the supplement experienced a significant improvement in memory.[10]

Using PS, combined with omega-3 supplements, may also aid in the treatment of ADHD and mood in children. In another study, 200 children with ADHD were assigned to 15 weeks of treatment with either a placebo or supplements containing PS and omega-3. Study results revealed that participants taking the supplements had a significant improvement in mood and a reduction in ADHD behavior when compared to those given the placebo.[11]

In another study with 36 kids ranging in age between 4 and 14 years, Phosphatidylserine (PS) was shown to improve a greater spectrum of symptoms than commonly prescribed ADHD drugs. The children were randomly assigned to receive either 200 mg a day of PS or placebo for two months. The results showed that PS produced significant improvements in attention, hyperactivity, impulsive behaviors and short-term auditory memory.[12]

CHAPTER ELEVEN

Homeopathy and Body Work Can Heal Concussions

At the University of California, studies show that children who have a history of a concussion are more likely to develop ADHD and have difficulty controlling their moods.[1] When ADHD is caused by a concussion, physical injury, a shock to the head or a shock to the base of the spine, then natural supplements are not always enough. Homeopathy and various forms of bodywork can make the difference. Because my ADHD and Parkinson's disease were caused by four major concussions earlier in my life, both homeopathy and bodywork were also a big part of healing my brain injuries.

Homeopathy is a form of medicine approved by the FDA that does not involve the of use drugs. Specific homeopathic remedies can awaken your body's ability to heal the brain, while supplements provide the necessary nutritional support for that to happen. In simple terms, homeopathic remedies turn on your body's healing genes.

Homeopathy is often discredited and attacked by the American Medical Establishment on the grounds that western science cannot determine how it works. In spite of tremendous opposition, it continues to be approved by the FDA because it has worked in many cases when drugs have not. One of its great benefits is that when it works, it has no side effects.

One of its drawbacks is that it does not always work. It doesn't always work for three reasons.

1. The wrong remedy is used.
2. The modern diet is deficient in the necessary minerals for the activated genes to do their job.
3. High stimulation tends to interfere with its effectiveness.

Two hundred years ago, homeopathy was most effective before the invention of stimulant drugs and junk food. Patients at that time were instructed to avoid the high stimulation of coffee for the treatments to work. Today, homeopathic remedies are less effective due to the common use of coffee, prescribed stimulant drugs and the high consumption of sugar and junk foods along with the fast pace of life, traffic, TV, video games, cell phones, email, etc. By limiting or abstaining from this hyper-stimulation and taking extra mineral supplements, homeopathic remedies can be most effective.

To heal a concussion, decreasing hyper-stimulation and getting extra mineral support is the first step. Homeopathy is the second. Yet, turning on your healing genes with homeopathy is still not enough. When a physical shock to the body causes oxidative stress, a physical resetting of the body may also be required. The most obvious example of this is a broken bone. For a broken bone to heal straight, it must be reset. Chiropractic bodywork can physically reset your brain's connection to the rest of the body.

When a physical shock causes the oxidative stress,
then a physical resetting of the body is required.

One of my readers, an Olympic medalist, shared with me that after many falls while skating, she developed the symptoms of depression, anxiety and ADHD. In her case, chiropractic care and my nutritional protocols were helpful but not enough. She also followed an inexpensive, six-week homeopathic brain function treatment, developed by Dr. Solar Farahmand, and most of her symptoms went away. When she repeated the program again, all of her symptoms disappeared. It was truly a miracle. I also personally benefited from this program. For more information about this homeopathic treatment go to http://www.homeopathicwonders.com.

Teaching workshops at a variety of conferences around the world, I have also heard miraculous testimonials regarding the benefits received from chiropractic care. Anyone who has ever had a rib out of joint knows what immediate relief you can feel after visiting a chiropractor. You can take all the pain pills in the world but the pain will continue until the rib is physically put back in place. Sometimes all it takes is a simple adjustment.

You can take pain pills
but the pain will continue
until the rib is physically put back in place.

When I was 14 years old, after my second major concussion, ten treatments with my chiropractor took away my terrible headaches. My chiropractor was also skilled in cranial-sacral therapy, which is also beneficial for healing the brain after a shock or concussion.

Later in life, as a result of more concussions, I developed chronic neck tension. Using the Anat Baniel Method (ABM) I was able to release my neck tension in one session. This unique approach was originally developed by Dr. Feldenkrais and then later advanced by Dr. Anat Baniel.

The Anat Baniel Method looks like a kind of bodywork, but it is really an innovative form of brainwork. By moving the body in slow, new and specific ways, the traumatized brain is activated and can actually learn to heal itself. In many cases, I have witnessed children with severe brain injuries from birth begin to speak and walk in a few treatments. For more information about ABM, visit http://www.anatbanielmethod.com/

With ABM, the traumatized brain is activated
and can actually learn to heal itself.

Due to recent lawsuits against the NFL, the long-term effects of concussions are finally coming into the light of public awareness. 4,000 former football players have filed lawsuits. Older athletes, who suffered from concussions while playing football, are experiencing symptoms similar to Parkinson's as well as memory loss and ADHD later in life.[2] In addition, the Army is now faced with over 500,000 soldiers returning back from battle with mild traumatic brain injury or TBI. Mild TBI is the new medical term to describe concussion.

Over 500,000 soldiers
have returned home
with mild traumatic brain injury.

TBI is called the "signature wound" of the war in Iraq and Afghanistan because it is the most common wound. Vets suffer from brain injury after exposure to improvised explosive devices (IEDs), a regular event for troops traveling the roads in Iraq and Afghanistan. This injury from exposure to a shock wave stimulates ongoing chronic oxidative stress in the brain. This has not only caused classic symptoms of ADHD but also depression, anxiety and dramatically high rates of suicide.

Most patients are unaware that they have sustained a concussion or that they are developing symptoms of ADHD. You can have a concussion and not blackout. Another problem with TBI is that sometimes the symptoms show up right away and at other times they don't. When symptoms develop later, a patient may not connect their symptoms with a head injury. This is especially true when symptoms develop days or months later.

You can have a concussion and not blackout
and symptoms may only show up six months later.

Typical symptoms of TBI are headache and a variety of other symptoms that directly correspond to many of the different symptoms of ADHD. They include:

1. ADHD distracted type: difficulty concentrating and slower reaction times.
2. ADHD sensitive type: nausea and difficulty with bright lights and sounds.
3. ADHD impulsive type: irritability and restlessness.
4. ADHD compulsive type: either insomnia or sleeping more.

Because of these symptoms, after a concussion or accident, students may suffer a drop in their grades, while adults may experience poor work performance. Research at the University of California found that ten percent of kids had a full depressive disorder six months after a concussion.[3] Yet, sometimes within hours after a brain injury, a child who has never been depressed before, is suddenly depressed and suicidal.

After a concussion, about ten percent of kids
had a full depressive disorder six months later.

In November of 2007, at a special conference for American military leaders, I was warmly invited to speak about the need for more relationship skills for our soldiers returning home from war. During that "top secret" conference, they were primarily discussing a new problem the military was facing…mild traumatic brain injury. It was reported that merely standing in a building or home, two football fields away from an IED explosion could cause traumatic brain injury. This was a new problem and they were looking for answers. They were also developing tests to better diagnose TBI because most soldiers did not know they had it.

One of the symptoms of TBI
is not knowing you have it.

At a dinner party with top brass, I was excited to share my insights about natural solutions. I shared how my four major concussions had caused my ADHD and later Parkinson's and how I had healed them. I was offering them the solution on a silver platter. Unfortunately, the top Army brass was "officially" not interested in my suggestions unless their doctors approved of it or it involved prescribed drugs.

Since that time, the America Defense Department has still not officially approved any new treatments for healing mild traumatic brain injury. Instead, they treat the symptoms with sleeping pills and antidepressants. This kind of treatment only delays the healing process.

In the past, the standard medical procedure was only to monitor a person who has experienced a concussion to see if something else, which is treatable, shows up. It was assumed that the brain will recover at its own pace within 7 to 10 days.

This oversight is finally being corrected. It is now recognized by the Army that soldiers with mild traumatic brain injury or TBI can be directly affected for three to six months and it may extend even further as is now being recognized with football players. Unfortunately, their solution is still to assume that the brain will recover at its own pace.

Soldiers with mild traumatic brain injury or TBI can be directly affected for three to six months.

While modern medicine has no remedies, homeopathy has over twenty FDA-approved remedies. One well-designed double-blind study has demonstrated homeopathy's effectiveness in treating concussions.[5]

Emotional Freedom Technique (EFT) has also shown tremendous benefits for soldiers with TBI and PTSD. EFT reduces anxiety and stress by identifying negative thought pattern and painful emotions while simply tapping a specific series of acupuncture points. In one study, 90% of soldiers practicing EFT no longer met the criteria for clinical PTSD compared with only 4% of the control group.[6] This same tool has been helpful for children, teens and adults with ADHD.

Even today, the standard medical treatment for both concussion and mild traumatic brain injury is merely physical and mental rest. For physical rest, patients are encouraged to stop playing sports and disengage from active duty until they are free of symptoms. For mental rest, they are required to refrain from reading, looking at a computer screen or doing homework. While this rest creates the opportunity for healing, it is natural solutions like Homeopathy, Chiropractic Care, Cranial-sacral Therapy, Anat Baniel Method or Emotional Freedom Technique along with extra nutrition that can deliver the results.

It is appalling that the only remedy modern medicine has for a concussion and the oxidative stress that results is simply to rest and avoid stimulation for six months. Try that with a 12-year-old boy who suffers from ADHD or severe learning challenges due to a concussion.

CHAPTER TWELVE

HT Therapy for Healing Oxidative Stress

Beside eating healthy foods and using supplements to increase glutathione and heal ADHD, there are also powerful ancient spa therapies that can increase the production of glutathione and heal the brain.

HT Therapy for reducing oxidative stress combines hydrotherapy, the use of mineral waters, along with hyperthermia, the use of heat, to induce a low fever in the brain. HT Therapy stands for hydrothermal therapy.

HT Therapy for healing oxidative stress in the brain originates in Germany, a country well known for respecting the healing power of spa treatments. For example, even today German health insurance gives heart disease patients a choice: they can receive drugs for heart disease or they can take a two-week trip to a German spa for hydrotherapy.[1] Both have been proven to help, but unlike the drugs, the spa has no negative side effects.

**For treating heart disease,
health insurance in Germany pays for spa treatments.**

This ancient German HT Therapy is the most powerful therapy available for oxidative stress and yet very little clinical research has been done on it. Because it can be easily self-administered and done at home, there is not enough profit for the business of healthcare to support peer-reviewed scientific research. In my Mars Venus Wellness Center, for ten years we used HT Therapy extensively. When combined with extra nutritional support, HT Therapy produced tremendous benefits for nearly every health challenge.

Because HT Therapy can be
easily self-administered and done at home,
there is little research to validate its benefits.

Recently, in 2013, one clinical study was done with 40 autistic children.[2] Researchers found just one 30-minute bath, at 102 degrees Fahrenheit , helped soothe the symptoms of autism and made the children more sociable. It improved their ability to communicate and made them less prone to repeating the same action over and over. What is most significant in this study is that these changes did not occur when the bath was only a few degrees cooler at 98 degrees Fahrenheit. A hot bath worked while a warm bath did not. This study shows only a fraction of what can be done with a bath treatment if it is done consistently every other day for three months.

This study shows only a fraction of what can be done
with HT Therapy every other day.

Hundreds of years ago, hydrothermal therapy was called "the cure when nothing else worked." It involves taking a bath for an hour, lying down on your back with your face above water but with the rest of your head underwater. While maintaining this position, the water temperature is gradually increased so that during the last 20 minutes, the water temperature is around 103 degrees Fahrenheit. This water temperature generates a low fever in the brain to neutralize oxidative stress.

**Hydrothermal therapy was called
"the cure when nothing else worked."**

During the first 20 minutes, the water can be between 97 and 101 degrees Fahrenheit. During the second twenty minutes, the water can be 101 degrees Fahrenheit or slightly above. In the last twenty minutes, the water temperature is maintained at 103 degrees Fahrenheit. All temperatures and timing are approximate.

With supervision, this can be done at home in a bathtub. Just add two cups of Epsom salt to the water. Even better add a cup of magnesium chloride to the bath. At other times, add special clays known to facilitate detoxification. It is fine to occasionally sit up when it gets a little boring or if you wish to drink some cold water. If your bathtub is not long enough, then simply bend your knees.

This process is completely safe for all ages and stages of life however, hot water therapy is not recommended when someone has a history of high blood pressure or Multiple Sclerosis (MS). For natural solutions to first support normal blood pressure and MS refer to **MarsVenus.com/blood-pressure** or **MarsVenus. com/MS**.

For people with high blood pressure or MS, this procedure can be done at lower temperatures in addition to taking vitamin C and glutathione supplements. Great health benefits will be achieved.

This protocol is to be repeated every other day for three months. Keeping the head partially underwater allows the temperature of the brain to increase. This induced fever in the brain kills harmful bacteria and inhibits viral replication. In addition, during a fever, more immune factors are released to heal the brain.[3] Infrared saunas are also very helpful for detoxification and inducing a fever but not as powerful as HT Therapy.

**During a fever,
more immune factors are released.**

Using this method for three months, I witnessed the complete healing of a seven-year-old autistic boy. At my wellness center, parents of autistic children noticed tremendous and lasting improvement in their children after a few days of this treatment. Ten years later, I closed the center because parents could do the treatments at home and didn't need to travel to northern California. A TV documentary of this treatment was shown on the news in the San Francisco Bay Area.

Even without HT Therapy, fevers from sickness are very beneficial for the brain. For many years, mothers of autistic children have reported that during a fever, their children's symptoms of autism have disappeared only to reappear after the fever is over.[4] The symptoms come back because the infection has not been fully healed. More than 80% of children in one study of 30 children with autism spectrum disorders showed improvement in behavior during temperature elevations.[5]

**Even without HT Therapy, fevers
from sickness are very beneficial for the brain.**

Doing HT therapy every other day gives your immune system the support it needs to finally rid the brain of the chronic infection that is associated with all mental challenges from ADHD to autism. After just two weeks following this procedure, many of my clients have reported tremendous clarity, calm and focus.

HT Therapy can bring clarity, calm and focus

even when only practiced a few times.

Many people resist lying in a bath for one hour because they become too bored. An easy remedy for this is listening to music or a book on tape using an underwater MP3 player and speaker. For more information about this, search for a FINIS Neptune Underwater MP3 player at Amazon.com.

Another remedy for overcoming resistance to this treatment is to follow the basic protocol with shorter times or watch a video while sitting up without putting the head underwater. The results will be less but they will be significant. With that improvement, you can gradually move into keeping your head underwater.

Even if your child is not willing to put their head partially under water to keep the heat in, they will still get tremendous benefit from simply sitting in the bathtub for one hour if possible. Make sure the last twenty minutes is at 103 degrees Fahrenheit. When done at night before bed, this can also help improve the quality of their sleep as well.

When done at night before bed,
HHT can improve the quality of sleep.

It is always good at first to have children start the therapy sitting up. Then after a few sessions, as they become accustomed to sitting for an hour, introduce the idea of lying back in the water.

There can be many variations of HT Therapy. Even taking a cold shower every day after your normal shower will increase glutathione production in the liver. After taking a cold shower or bath, your body reacts by producing an internal fever to warm up.

When I was a young monk living in Switzerland, I would start each day with a brief, but very cold bath. During those years I was never sick and all of my childhood allergies went away. Years later, after I was no longer a monk or taking cold baths, my allergies returned.

As a young monk living in Switzerland, starting each day with a brief, but very cold bath eliminated my childhood allergies.

Young Tibetan monks generate this internal fever by practicing meditation while sitting outside in the snow in sub-zero temperatures wearing little more than a loin-cloth. They are able to generate enough body heat to melt the snow around them. This internal fever induced by exposure to the cold increases the production of glutathione. Scandinavian clubs of men and women who regularly swim in the cold waters of the North Atlantic Ocean during winter are known for their vitality, health and longevity.

The internal fever induced by exposure to the cold increases the production of glutathione.

At my wellness center, to maximize the benefits of HT therapy, following the bath treatment we would sit in a Far Infrared Sauna for twenty to thirty minutes. These low-heat saunas have proven to be much more efficient than the traditional high-heat saunas. Even young autistic children enjoyed sitting in them. The Far Infrared Sauna has a three-fold benefit with or without HT therapy. The benefits are:

1. Increased sweating which helps to detoxify harmful mercury and other heavy metals. This is particularly helpful when a child or adult has deficiencies in glutathione.

2. An induced mild fever, which kills bacteria infections and increases immune factors to reduce oxidative stress in the brain.

3. Increased circulation to provide more nutrients to the brain.

Another therapy besides far infrared sauna that provides similar support is lying on a BioMat. This special mat manufactured by Richway, combines far infrared heat with amethyst crystals to raise the body temperature inducing a low fever. Combined with the elimination of toxins and waste produced by the sweating, oxidative stress is minimized.

Chapter Thirteen

Elimination Diets
Can Reverse ADHD

The FDA lists over 33 double-blind clinical trials demonstrating that artificial food colors are related to ADHD and other childhood related problem behaviors.[1] Because ADHD is directly related to digestion and food allergies, by eliminating certain foods, dramatic improvements have been observed. Food allergies and indigestion trigger inflammation in the brain, which results in different degrees of ADHD.[2]

The most well-known elimination diet proven to reverse ADHD 50% of the time is the Feingold Diet.[3] It gets great results by eliminating foods with artificial colors, artificial flavors, several preservatives, synthetic sweeteners and salicylate (aspirin-like) foods. The bad news is that many of the foods found in the supermarket are taboo, but the good news is that there are safe, natural versions for nearly all problem foods. After eliminating these processed foods for four days, you can reintroduce them to test each one to see if it causes problems. To learn more about the Feingold Diet, visit **https://www.feingold.org**.

Other elimination diets include testing for food allergies that may be causing ADHD. The usual food allergies are with the foods we most commonly eat:

1. Bread (and other gluten products)
2. Sugar (and all sugar substitutes be they natural or artificial)
3. Corn (particularly GMO)
4. Dairy (pasteurized)
5. Soy (GMO and unfermented)
6. Artificial food colors, sweeteners and additives

Eliminating these foods and artificial food colorings and additives quickly helps the majority of children lose their symptoms of ADHD.[4] After removing these foods for four days, you can begin to test each one to see if the symptoms return. If symptoms return with a particular food, then it must be eliminated for some time longer. In some cases, after abstaining from a particular food, it can be reintroduced in moderation without triggering symptoms.

> **Eliminating bread, sugar, corn, dairy and soy**
> **can dramatically improve**
> **digestion and increase focus.**

There is a definite link between gut health, digestion and ADHD. Food sensitivities and allergies cause indigestion and inflammation in the gut. This directly inhibits healthy brain performance. Almost 90 percent of children with autism and ADHD have some degree of chronic colitis.[5] Gut health and good digestion is necessary for a healthy brain. A variety of naturopathic doctors treat children with ADHD and autism using a multimodal approach by supporting digestion and detoxification along with nutritional supplementation.

A more restrictive program for healing gut inflammation is the GAPS program. This program may take a couple of years but it has been a lifesaver for thousands of people suffering from severe irritable bowel syndrome, Chron's Disease and other intestinal challenges. Dr. Campbell-McBride developed the GAPS program and used it to cure her three-year-old son's autism.[6]

**Gut health and digestion
are necessary for a healthy brain.**

Healthy digestion is a big part of healing ADHD and may take many months or years. However, without fully healing the gut, you can still begin to heal the brain because vitamin, mineral and amino acid supplementation do not depend on a healthy digestive system.

Sometimes, we can completely eliminate ADHD symptoms by reducing sugar products and taking a few extra supplements. With extra vitamin C, grape seed extract, special mineral orotates and natural amino acid support it is relatively easy to do. This protocol is explained more fully in Appendix One.

By first supporting healthy brain function, stress levels decrease and the gut can begin to heal. Once stress levels drop, then following specific protocols for healing the gut can be more productive. I have seen this process increase focus and positive moods within days for hundreds of children and adults with ADHD. Details of this simplified program are outlined at **MarsVenus.com/ADHD**.

Healing Food Allergies
Improves Brain Performance

An alternative approach to elimination diets is to directly heal the gut and heal food allergies. Rather than avoid the allergen, heal the allergy. Your body has 10 trillion cells. By strengthening the cell membrane potential to protect it from allergens, your allergies may go away. I had allergies my whole life and eventually healed them with natural solutions. A greater understanding for healing allergies is available at **MarsVenus.com/allergies**.

Even if you heal your allergies, genetically modified foods (GMOs) are simply indigestible and toxic to the body. Toxic foods inhibit gut, liver and brain function, which in turn trigger a variety of ADHD symptoms.

As stated before, the most toxic foods are genetically modified soy and corn, processed wheat or gluten products, excessive sugar and pasteurized milk (as opposed to raw milk, butter, yogurt, kefir or undenatured milk proteins). If meat and dairy products are not labeled organic, then the animals were fed GMO soy and corn, which makes their meat toxic as well.

A healthy body can tolerate some degree of these toxic foods but they will definitely interfere with the body's ability to heal itself. I hope you will support all legislation to label GMO foods, which is only the first step to eliminating them. To get a list of GMO free foods you can go to http://www.nongmoproject.org.

**Even if you heal your allergies,
genetically modified foods (GMOs) are
still toxic to the body.**

"Cheerios" and "Grape Nuts" are the first big cereal brands to label their boxes "GMO free." They are setting a precedent; if their sales go up, others will follow. Whole Foods Market is planning to voluntarily label all foods that are GMO. If GMO foods are to be legal, at the very least, we all deserve the right to know what we are eating and the freedom to choose. GMO companies are thriving because they spend millions on misleading advertising to prevent mandatory GMO labeling. Although they spend millions to lobby Congress, you can still make a difference. Every purchase you make counts as a meaningful vote for change. No more GMOs.

You can't always avoid toxic substances, but you can help your body fight them off. In Book Three of this series, *Staying Focused In A Hyper World: Super Fuel To Relax And Recharge Your Brainpower*, we will explore foods, supplements and detoxification protocols to help you win this battle and achieve optimal brain performance and lasting health.

But first, in Book Two, *Staying Focused In A Hyper World: Decreasing Stress To Increase Happiness, Passion And Vitality*, we will explore the many faces and stages of ADHD in your life, work and relationships. Understanding your particular symptoms can help you determine the right natural solution for you or your children.

Can Your Doctor Help?

With hundreds of studies demonstrating the effectiveness of nutritional supplementation for ADHD, it is shocking to me that this information is not more widely available.

You will get over a million results on the Internet if you search "non-drug solutions for ADHD". But after reading hundreds of suggestions and studies on natural solutions, it is easy to feel overwhelmed. With so many choices, most parents feel unqualified to make a decision that could affect the wellbeing of their child.

**There are so many natural solutions that
it can be hard to pick the right one for you.**

With so many options, it is definitely tempting to ask your friendly doctor and let them decide. However, they may not be much help because they are only trained to give drugs. Most doctors, unless they are also naturopaths, have received only a few hours of general nutritional training.

**Feeling unqualified to pick a natural solution,
parents often seek the advice of a doctor
who may know even less.**

Without any training in nutrition, doctors commonly discount the effectiveness of natural solutions for ADHD. They casually minimize the side effects of taking stimulant drugs and even worse, they know very little about the long-term side effects. If you wish to consult a doctor, always get a second opinion and make sure they are holistic practitioners with a history of success using natural solutions. With so many new resources and natural solutions, you can heal ADHD, improve your memory and increase your brain performance on your own.

**You can achieve optimal brain function and focus
with the right natural program.**

It is not a one solution fits all, in Book One of *Staying Focused In A Hyper World*, we have explored the natural solutions to heal the brain. In Book Two of *Staying Focused In A Hyper World*, we will explore the three action steps to develop new patterns of self-expression and interaction by transforming old automatic reactions, patterns and addictions. You will gain the insight you and your children need to lower stress and increase happiness, passion and vitality. To order Book Two of *Staying Focused In A Hyper World* go to **MarsVenus.com/book-two**.

In Book Three of *Staying Focused In A Hyper World*, you will learn how to sustain your transformation with a healthy diet, which includes super foods to relax and restore your brainpower. You will learn what supplements work and why they do. You will learn what food to eat and what to avoid. To order Book Three of *Staying Focused In A Hyper World* go to **MarsVenus.com/book-three**.

If your child has some of the more challenging symptoms of Autistic Spectrum Disorder, I suggest reading my book *Lost And Found, Natural Solutions for Autism Spectrum Disorder*. Many of the causes are similar to what causes ADHD but the solutions are more diet related and therapies are more extensive. This book is also a must read for every mother preparing to have a child. To order *Lost and Found*, go to **MarsVenus.com/autism-book**.

Living an Extraordinary Life

Healing the brain and living an extraordinary life is a big and complex subject. I have written this book to help simplify the journey and provide real choices. By understanding the various causes of oxidative stress, the one brain condition that gives rise to ADHD, you have the necessary insight to determine the best natural solution for you and your family.

The good news with natural solutions is there are no negative side effects. The worst they can do is not work until you find the right one. While this is not always an easy journey, you now have the necessary insight to discover what will work for you. I do not know what will work for you, but I would like to know. Please keep us updated with your progress.

Always remember you are not alone on this journey. Join me at MarsVenus.com for down to earth advice on life and love. Share your experiences with natural solutions. Your successes will inspire others to find the right solutions for them. May you and your family enjoy a lifetime of health, happiness and lasting love.

APPENDIX ONE

Good, Better and
Best Suggested Protocols

Throughout *Staying Focused In A Hyper World*, we have explored in depth, the many causes of oxidative stress and a variety of protocols for both protecting your brain and healing it. In working with thousands of clients over the past 12 years, I have seen some protocols work for some and not for others. In some cases, the easiest protocols produced immediate benefits. In other cases, the solution was more complex, or at least took more time.

Keep in mind that self-healing is not an exact science. It is a journey of finding out what works for you. Knowing the many options for healing ADHD does not mean you have to try them all. There are always many ways to heal the same condition. If you were to travel to a destination, there are hundreds of different ways to go.

**Knowing the many options for healing ADHD
does not mean you have to try them all.**

Nature provides a variety of healing solutions for any one condition. At a conference of seasoned naturopathic doctors, they were requested to write out a protocol for a particular stated condition. Not one out of a hundred doctors gave the same protocol, yet they had all previously witnessed their protocol work in their practice.

I have listed below a variety of simple protocols to begin your journey of finding out what will work for you. They are designed to fit your particular budget as well as your willingness to take supplements.

The thought of taking nine to twelve pills for some people seems unthinkable, while it is perfectly acceptable for others. In the beginning, I had a resistance to taking a lot of pills, until I discovered that a friend, who was thirty years older than me, took over ten pills, three times a day. Unlike most people his age, he was not taking any prescribed drugs and he was vibrant and healthy. It changed my whole perspective. Somehow, I was thinking that only sick people take a lot of pills. My thinking changed that day to a more expanded perspective: sick people take lots of drugs, while healthy people have the wisdom to supplement a good diet with extra nutrition.

We mistakenly think
only sick people take a lot of pills.

When taking supplements, it is important to see them not as drugs with dangerous side effects but as the missing ingredients from the food we eat. Just as you might add a long list of spices to make a meal more tasty and healthy, you can now add a list of supplements to make it more nutritious. With the Mars Venus Super Food Shake and Mars Venus Super Minerals, I personally don't need to take as many supplements because they contain most of the missing nutrients needed for optimal brain performance.

In most cases, these supplements are simply concentrated nutrients that we would normally find in a meal if our food was not so processed or nutrient deficient. Just as food is necessary for both adults and children, supplements are now necessary as well. There is so much misinformation about supplements that some parents are concerned about their children taking natural supplements when every day they do not question what is in a bowl of cereal, macaroni and cheese, a milk shake and French fries, a soft drink, ice cream or any of the millions of packaged foods purchased every day which are filled with chemicals and neurotoxins. Unlike the many processed foods commonly eaten by our children, the supplements I recommend are completely healthy. They are non-toxic in the suggested doses and are completely safe to take.

Supplements are simply concentrated nutrients that we would normally find in a meal if our food was not so processed or nutrient deficient.

In almost all cases, if you are already taking certain supplements, they will not interfere with the suggestions below. If you are not noticing much with your current supplement use, you may wish to temporarily discontinue them to see if the suggestions below can make a bigger difference. Then you may introduce them again and see if they add to your benefits.

In all cases, the suggested doses are for adults. Since natural supplements are basically the nutrients missing from healthy foods and not drugs they are also great for children but the doses should be proportionately less. For children, who are not yet able to swallow pills, the capsules can be opened and then added to the super food shake or any healthy drink.

For children, who are not yet able to swallow pills, the capsules can be opened and then added to the super food shake.

To find the right dose for your children consider the suggested doses are for someone 100 to 200 pounds. So if your children are in the range of 50 to 100 pounds they would benefit from half doses. From 25 to 50 pounds they would require a fourth dose. Keep in mind that these suggestions are always approximate and do not have to be exact since these natural supplements have no side effects. They are not drugs with potentially dangerous side effects.

These protocols are designed to be a simple and clear starting off place for you. You can then tailor your supplement use according to what works for you. If they are working, you should notice results in days or weeks. If they don't work, you may need to add more of the other supplements to complement what you are doing.

> **Taking supplements is not an exact science,**
> **tailor your supplement use**
> **according to what works for you.**

There are many different causes of the oxidative stress that gives rise to you or your children's symptoms. Depending on the cause or a combination of causes, different solutions will be required. We will explore a more tailored approach in Appendix Two and Three. Appendix One is a summary of the most important natural supplements in a simple solution. It is designed to assist you in creating an easy plan of action for you or your children.

In the following protocols, sometimes I suggest particular brands of nutrients because I have worked with them and find them to be both economical and effective. Other brands may or may not be equally effective. A more detailed explanation describing each of these nutrients can be found at **MarsVenus. com/supplements**.

To heal the basic oxidative stress that gives rise to ADHD and improve memory and focus, I have divided my best suggestions into three categories of Good, Better and Best. In Appendix Two, I suggest additional supplements according to your temperament. In Appendix Three, I have additional suggestions if the cause of your ADHD is more complicated like blood sugar issues, adrenal burnout, irritable bowel, etc. And finally, in Appendix Four, I suggest some additional practical tips for resetting your brain and body to achieve optimal brain performance.

This is a list of protocols that I have personally seen to work. It is best to take the suggested supplements 10-20 minutes before meals. If you forget or this is not possible, they can be taken during or after a meal. They will still work but be a little less effective. If taking a supplement on an empty stomach causes any discomfort, then take with meals.

> **If taking a supplement on an empty stomach**
> **causes any discomfort, then take with meals.**

If you take too much of a supplement, the side effect will only be the slight discomfort of a headache, stomachache or mild diarrhea. In this case, there is nothing to worry about. If you feel nauseous or have a headache, try taking your supplements with a meal. If discomfort still persists, then lower the dose. To find the right dose for you, stop for a couple of days and then resume with a dose lower than what you were taking. Follow this procedure until discomfort goes away. For more information about each suggested supplement, visit **MarsVenus.com/supplements.**

Good:

Protocol 1. The easiest and most inexpensive, which produces immediate focus for many people. This program includes only 6 supplements. As you experience results, you may be able to cut the dose in half. After you recognize the benefits, use as needed.

1. Take one-half teaspoon of **Liposomal Vitamin C** twice daily. For children or adults who prefer a vitamin C drink that tastes like fruit punch, combine liposomal Vitamin C with **Catie's Whole Food Vitamin C Plus**.
2. Take two capsules of **Grape Seed Extract** twice daily.
3. Take two **Super Minerals** twice daily (ionic trace minerals and mineral orotates). Start with one a day and gradually increase to two capsules, twice a day. These minerals support brain performance but also detoxify heavy metals from the brain. Too much detoxification may cause a temporary headache or slight head pressure. After taking one, if you don't have a headache or slight head pressure that day then increase by one capsule each day up to four a day. At times of great stress, you can increase the dose as needed up to two capsules, three times a day.
4. Take one tablet of **Omega-3** twice daily. A powerful liquid source of Omega-3 for children who don't take capsules is **Liposomal DHA**.
5. Take one **Potential multivitamin** twice daily.
6. Approximately one capsule of **Berberine** before every meal.

Better:

Protocol 2: The most effective protocol for focus, mental flexibility and positive mood. This program includes eight supplements twice a day and a Super Foods Shake for breakfast. After you experience results, you may cut the doses in half. So, if you are taking one dose a day of a particular supplement, then take one dose approximately every other day. Use as needed. For more information about each suggested supplement, visit **MarsVenus. com/supplements.**

1. Follow the guidelines for Protocol 1 above and add the following nutritional supplements.
2. Mix two scoops of the **Mars Venus Super Foods** meal replacement shake with a little fruit (one half a banana or berries) and eight ounces of water or almond milk.
3. Take one time-released **multi-B vitamin**.
4. Take one **digestive enzyme** 10-20 minutes before your morning Super Foods Shake and before each meal.
5. Take one capsule of **2-AEP Membrane Complex** 10-20 minutes before each meal to repair cell membranes and balance blood sugar.
6. Take one capsules of **Phosphatidylserine** (PS) 10-20 minutes before each meal to support the fluidity of cell membranes.

Alternative Protocol 2: For a dairy free alternative to Protocol 2, instead of using the Mars Venus Super Foods Shake as your protein source, use the following non-dairy amino acid supplements. It's important to know that many people who are sensitive to dairy can digest the undenatured dairy in the Mars Venus Super Foods

Shake. This program includes nine additional supplements. After you experience results, you may cut the doses in half. Use as needed.

1. Follow the guidelines for Protocol 1 above and add the following nutritional supplements.
2. A morning shake with one scoop of **Collagen Peptides**, one tablespoon of **MCT Oil**, a handful of Goji berries and half a banana with some natural vanilla flavor added. Note: Gradually increase MCT Oil to the maximum dose of one tablespoon. Decrease dose if bloating or pain occurs due to candida die-off. Then gradually increase again.
3. Take one capsule of **L-Tyrosine** 10-20 minutes before each meal.
4. Take one capsule **5-HTP** 10-20 minutes before each meal.
5. Take one capsule **NAC** (N-Acetyl-Cysteine) 10-20 minutes before each meal.
6. Take one time-released **multi-B vitamin** with breakfast.
7. Take one **digestive enzyme** 10-20 minutes before each meal.
8. Take one capsule of **2-AEP Membrane Complex** 10-20 minutes before each meal to repair cell membranes.
9. Take one capsules of **Phosphatidylserine** (PS) 10-20 minutes before each meal to support the fluidity of cell membranes.

Best:

Protocol 3. The most effective protocol for focus, memory, mental flexibility and positive mood if you are irritable, stressed, moody or have the tendency to feel depressed. This protocol includes five additional supplements and my favorite Lemon Cleanse Drink before a Super Foods Shake for breakfast. After you experience results, you may cut the doses in half. So, if you are taking one pill a day, then take one pill approximately every other day. Use as needed. For more information about each suggested supplement, visit **MarsVenus.com/supplements.**

1. Make a special Lemon Cleanse Drink and drink 20 minutes before your morning Mars Venus Super Foods protein shake. Mix together the following ingredients:
   - One teaspoon of the **Mars Venus Super Cleanse**
   - One teaspoon of **Probiotics**
   - One scoop of **Collagen Peptides**
2. Follow the suggestions of Protocol 2 or Alternative Protocol 2.
3. Add one teaspoon of **MCT Oil** to the Mars Venus Shake. Gradually increase MCT Oil to maximum dose of one tablespoon. Decrease dose if bloating or pain occurs due to candida die-off. Then gradually increase again.
4. Take one capsule of **Lithium Orotate** twice daily. Once you feel more stable self-regulate this dose according to how you feel or how stressed you are. Reduce when you are feeling good and increase back up to two a day when you are feeling really stressed or down.
5. Take one **Brain Sharpener** twice daily. (Use Brain Sharpener for Kids for half dose.)

6. Take one **Hormone Balance** twice daily.
7. Take one **4-Endocrine** twice daily.
8. Take one-half teaspoon of **Liposomal Vitamin D3** twice daily.

APPENDIX TWO

Add On Supplements For Your Temperament

To get extra benefit for your temperament, the following supplements can be added to the Best Protocol in Appendix One. For children, simply cut the dose in half.

1. Creative Temperament

1. Cho-Wa Herbal Tea: This is the ultimate brain supplement for the creative and often distracted mind or anyone who feels a little tired after a meal. This cup of tea can be taken first thing in the morning or after breakfast or lunch. This brain tonic is particularly good for memory, energy, and sustaining focus. It contains 10 rejuvenating brain herbs. It can be used by all temperaments but is particularly helpful for the creative temperament.

2. Coconut Oil: Take one to three teaspoons of MCT Oil (concentrated oil from coconut) in your morning shake. It will convert to pure energy in your brain to keep you alert longer. Start with one teaspoon and gradually increase the dose every week as needed. This is particularly good when one has any blood sugar issues.

3. Resveratrol: Take one Resveratrol capsule in the morning to increase blood flow to brain and repair injured brain cells. This is

particularly good for lessening the effects of food sensitivi
is most commonly known for its anti-aging benefits.

4. Phosphatidylserine: Take one capsule of Phosphatidylserine
(PS) twice daily. This nutrient plays a major role in maintaining
the integrity of cell membranes, which in turn supports memory,
focus and clarity. For an even greater ability to stay organized,
take one capsule of **Brain Sharpener** twice daily. This powerful
supplement is a little more expensive but it is known to work
when nothing else works. It is all natural and made from 10
Chinese and Ayurvedic plants. It contains phosphatidylserine,
ginkgo, flax and Brahmi. (Use **Brain Sharpener for Kids** which
is a half the dose.)

2. Responsible Temperament

1. Magnesium: Most people are deficient in magnesium but particularly those with the responsible temperament. Take one capsule before bed to help relax and also be regular.

2. Ashwagandha: This herb helps the brain neurotransmitter
GABA do its job. It will help you to be more fluid, calm and flexible. In the **Serenity Formula**, Ashwagandha is combined with
Rhodiola extract for extra benefits. Rhodiola extract has been
shown to increase calm and focus. A more powerful form of
GABA (for adults only) is **Gabatrol** which can be used on special
occasions to remember what it feels like to be fully relaxed and
happy. Watch the video at **MarsVenus.com/Gabatrol** for instructions on its use.

3. Vitamin B: Take a time-released, multi-B vitamin. This will
keep you calm and relaxed during the day. Use as directed.

4. Taurine: This amino acid increases GABA to calm the brain and protects the brain from becoming overexcited. Take one capsule one to three times daily.

3. Bold Temperament

1. Collagen Peptides: When your muscles have to compete for the amino acids needed by your brain, you become unnecessarily restless. Collagen peptides support your muscles, which then provide extra energy and the amino acids needed to support your brain. Add one or two scoops to the **Mars Venus Super Foods Shake**.

2. Acetyl L-Carnitine: This amino acid is particularly helpful to convert fat into energy. It helps the body and brain to absorb and utilize the necessary omega-3 fats. Take one capsule twice daily.

3. Tongkat Ali: This herb is a natural super supplement to stimulate the production of testosterone. Men should take two capsules a day for five days and then take two days off. Women should take one capsule a day for five days and then take two days off. This helps to restore normal dopamine function along with increasing libido. Children can take half the dose without it affecting libido. It helps to counteract the testosterone suppressing effects of plastics and pesticides on both adults and children.

4. L-Carnosine: This amino acid is considered an ideal agent for treating and preventing degeneration from oxidative stress resulting from exercise or sugar consumption. It also stimulates circulation in the brain and neutralizes heavy metals.

4. Sensitive Temperament

1. 5-HTP: This amino acid supplement is the precursor to making serotonin. Women should take two capsules twice daily and men should take one capsule twice daily. This will help calm the brain and stabilize your positive mood.

2. Lithium Orotate: This important mineral helps to protect the brain from oxidative stress and also assists the brain in making more serotonin. It is already recommended in the "Best Protocol" in Appendix One. For the sensitive temperament with more extreme ups and downs, when coupled with two super minerals three times a day, they can take, as needed, up to three capsules a day.

3. Aloe Vera Polymannose (APMC): This extract of aloe and other polysaccharides provides incredible support for the gut, digestion and brain with extra support for the health of cell membranes. People who are overly sensitive often have extra thin cell walls and this natural supplement will strengthen the cell membrane thus reducing infection and inflammation. Take one capsule once or twice daily.

4. Optimized Saffron: This extract of **Saffron** has been known to improve serotonin production in the brain creating greater calm and optimism while decreasing addictive cravings for sugar and carbs. Take one capsule twice daily.

APPENDIX THREE

Add On Supplements For Your Specific Health Concerns

By addressing your health concerns with natural solutions you will not depend on over the counter or prescribed drugs that inhibit optimal brain function. Below is a list of "add on" supplements for specific health benefits. The suggested supplements or therapies listed below are prioritized with the most important and most economical supplements being listed first in each category.

You may wish to begin with one or two of these Add On Supplements to see if that is enough to get the benefits you seek. Depending on your budget or your situation, you may choose to try several at once. It is not always necessary to take all of them. More Add On Supplements may be needed depending on your age or the severity of your condition. The older we get, the more help we can use.

For example, because two of my siblings have dementia and I previously had Parkinson's Disease, I am particularly concerned about my memory. Every day, I follow Protocol Three (Best) in Appendix One but, as an extra precaution, I take most of the Add On Supplements listed below for memory. Occasionally, when I gain extra weight, I follow the protocol for weight loss. When I am feeling clear, energized, focused and healthy, I will often back off from taking any of these extra supplements.

Ideally, for best results, these "add on" supplements are to be added to any of the three suggested protocols in Appendix One and Appendix Two. Keep in mind that using any of the three protocols (Good, Better, Best) may be enough to address your condition. At other times or for different people, any or all of the suggested Add On Supplements in each category are most helpful.

Using any of the three protocols
may be enough to address your condition
without using the Add On Supplements.

Using these Add On Supplements without one of the three protocols (Good, Better, Best) listed in Appendix One will not be as effective. If one of the Add On Supplements is already included in the protocol that you pick, there is no need to repeat it.

If one of the Add On Supplements is already included
in the protocol that you pick (Good, Better, Best),
there is no need to repeat it.

Just as positive relationships are necessary to stimulate the production of healthy hormones and brain chemicals, for these natural supplements to work most effectively, a healthy diet and regular exercise is also necessary. The better your diet and exercise program, the less supplements you will need to take. While it is more difficult today to get healthy food, we can at least try to avoid the bad stuff. As for exercise, if you can walk, then you can easily get the exercise you need. A thirty-minute walk three to five times a week is the minimum for these supplements to be most effective.

**A thirty-minute walk three to five times
a week is the minimum
for these supplements to be most effective.**

Some of these natural solutions directly support optimal brain function, memory and help to heal ADHD, while others are designed to overcome common health challenges which directly influence your brain's ability to fully heal. By learning to restore normal health, you can at last be free from needing prescribed or over-the-counter drugs that inhibit your brain's ability to protect itself from oxidative stress and heal.

Each of the following solutions I have found to be helpful in healing various conditions. I share my insights for educational purposes only to assist you in determining the right course of action for you and your children. Most people are simply not aware of all the amazing natural solutions available. As mentioned before, these are not the only solutions for better health but I have seen them work again and again.

For most people, these Add On Supplements are for temporary use and not to be taken indefinitely. They are for healing while the protocols in Appendix One are designed to sustain your health.

In many cases, the Add On Supplements are only required for a few months. Once you are free from needing prescription drugs or addictive substances, the nutritional support from the three protocols in Appendix One are often enough to fully recharge your brainpower on a daily basis. You may then occasionally use your Add On Supplements when you need extra support.

Blood Sugar Issues
and Diabetes

High blood sugar is associated with low glutathione production. As we have already explored, glutathione is essential for brain health. For blood sugar issues and diabetes any or all of these suggestions may help. Depending on the severity of your condition, you may only need to apply a few of the suggestions below. For more information about each suggested supplement, visit **MarsVenus.com/supplements.** For more information about the causes of blood sugar issues, visit **MarsVenus.com/blood-sugar.**

1. Reduce or avoid drinking juices and soft drinks or eating simple carbohydrates, starches or breads.
2. Add one scoop of **PGX granules** to the **MarsVenus Super Foods** Shake. In addition, take one **PGX capsule** before meals. Drink with plenty of water and gradually increase dose according to the instructions on the bottle. Taking more than one capsule before meals without drinking with enough water may result in constipation.
3. Take one capsule of **2-AEP Membrane Complex** three times daily before each meal.
4. Take one capsule of **Berberine** three times daily before each meal.
5. Take one capsule of **4-Endocrine** three times daily before each meal. This herbal supplement is a little more expensive but it is very effective. It is all natural and contains extracts from fruits, vegetables and Ayurvedic and Chinese herbs.

Heavy Metal Detox and Weight Loss

As we have already explored, the diet of junk foods that leads to obesity increases a child's risk of ADHD and an adult's risk of developing cognitive impairment and dementia. Your body holds on to fat to store toxins. Through detoxification and weight loss, you can restore health to your body and brain. The program below can help detoxify the body and manage weight. For more information about each suggested product, visit **MarsVenus.com/ supplements**. For more information about detox and weight loss, visit **MarsVenus.com/weight-loss**.

1. Follow the suggestions for good, better and best protocols in Appendix One.
2. Avoid all juices and soft drinks, junk foods, simple carbohydrates, starches or breads.
3. For five days, limit your diet to one meal a day and for the other two meals, use the **Super Foods Shake** as a meal replacement. To increase fat burning, add one tablespoon of **MCT Oil** to your super food shake.
4. Make a special Lemon Cleanse Drink and drink 20 minutes before your morning Mars Venus Super Foods Shake. Mix together the following ingredients.
   - One teaspoon of the **Mars Venus Super Cleanse**
   - One teaspoon of **Probiotics**
   - One scoop of **Collagen Peptides**
5. After the first five days, begin a special two-day cleansing fast. Stop all solid foods and the Mars Venus Super Foods Shake. Enjoy the Lemon Cleanse Drink and 8 ounces of water for breakfast, mid-morning snack, lunch, snack in the afternoon and dinner. Continue to take suggested

supplements for any of the three protocols in Appendix One; Good, Better or Best.

6. Repeat this cycle for as long as necessary. On fasting days, drink at least an additional 4-6 glasses of purified water. As long as you have any extra weight, you can continue this program. Although it is mostly a liquid diet, you will get all the nutrition you require for optimal health.

7. Take **Zeolites** first thing in the morning and before bed daily for two months. This detoxifying mineral extract from volcanic rocks helps cleanse the brain of heavy metals, herbicides, pesticides and insecticides.

8. Take one capsule of **4-Constipation** before bed every night.

9. Use any of the above suggestions for blood sugar issues before your meal replacement shakes and meal.

Chronic Pain and Fibromyalgia

By using natural alternatives instead of over-the-counter pain pills, your body can make the necessary glutathione to recharge your brainpower and eventually heal the condition giving rise to pain. If you must take pain killers, then at least use these suggestions along with the pain killers. For chronic pain relief, any or all of these suggestions may help. These suggestions are not drugs, so they may take a few days or weeks to begin noticing results. Depending on the severity of your condition, you may only need to apply a few of the suggestions below. For more information, visit **MarsVenus.com/supplements** or **MarsVenus.com/pain-relief**.

1. Take one capsule of **Serrapeptase** once or twice daily. Start with one and take two if necessary.
2. Take one teaspoon **LiposomalCurcumin/Resveratrol** twice daily.
3. Take one capsule of **Astaxanthin** twice daily.
4. Take one capsule of **MSM** twice daily. This can gradually be doubled or tripled if more is needed.
5. Follow the Heavy Metal Detox and Weight Loss suggestions listed above until pain is gone.
6. Exercise for 10 minutes daily on a rebounder or practice the easy Isoflex exercises.
7. Take 150mg twice a day of DMG. Start with half dose and work up to full dose.

Memory Loss or ADHD
Caused by Pain Pills

If you have taken pain pills or other over-the-counter drugs in the past, any or all of these suggestions may help for memory loss and/or ADHD. These supplements help reduce oxidative stress in the gut and brain and assist your liver in making glutathione. Depending on the severity of your condition, you may only need to apply a few of the suggestions below. For more information, visit **MarsVenus.com/ supplements** or **MarsVenus.com/acetaminophen**.

1. Take three capsules of **Aloe Vera Polymannose Complex** twice daily for one month. Then reduce to two capsules twice daily for a month. Then use as needed.
2. Take one capsule of **Alpha-lipoic Acid** twice daily.
3. Take one capsule of **Resveratrol** twice daily.
4. Take three capsules of **Phosphatidylserine (PS)** twice daily. For increased benefit instead take three capsules of **Brain Sharpener** twice daily.
5. Take one capsule of **Berberine** daily before each meal.
6. Take one-half teaspoon of **Liposomal Vitamin C** twice daily.
7. Take one-half teaspoon of **Liposomal Glutathione** twice daily.
8. Take one-half teaspoon of **Liposomal Vitamin D3** twice daily.
9. Add two tablespoons of **Stabilized Rice Bran (Tocotrienols)** to your daily Super Foods Shake.
10. Take one capsule of **4-Constipation** before bed.

Advanced Cases of Memory Loss, Parkinson's, Dementia and Alzheimer's

For more advanced cases of memory loss, Parkinson's, dementia and Alzheimer's, any or all of these suggestions may help. These suggestions are most effective when added to Protocol 3 in Appendix One. For more information about each suggested product, visit **MarsVenus.com/supplements**. For more information about the causes and remedies for these advanced cases, visit **MarsVenus.com/advanced-memory-loss**. For many people, just the first three suggestions along with Protocol Three (Best) will be enough. This condition requires high doses of the first four suggested supplements. Once dramatic improvement occurs within a couple of weeks you can gradually reduce dosages as needed.

1. Take three capsules of **Brain Sharpener** three times daily.
2. Take three capsules of **Hormone Balance** three times daily.
3. Take three capsules of **4-Endocrine** three times daily.
4. Take one dropper of **Liposomal Methyl B12/Folate** three times daily.
5. Take one capsule **Berberine** daily 10-20 minutes before each meal.
6. Add one teaspoon of **MCT Oil** to the Mars Venus Super Foods Shake and gradually build up to 2 tablespoons.
7. Take one capsule of **NAC** 10-20 minutes before each meal..
8. Take one-half teaspoon of **Liposomal Glutathione** twice daily
9. Take one-half teaspoon of **Liposomal Vitamin C** twice daily.
10. Take one-half teaspoon of **Liposomal DHA** twice daily.
11. Take one-half teaspoon of **Liposomal vitamin D3** twice daily.
12. Take one capsule of **4-Constipation** before bed until completely regular.

More Energy and Adrenal Support

Without adrenal support, healthy brain function is inhibited. For extra energy and adrenal support, any or all of these suggestions may help. Chronic fatigue is often caused by an exhausted adrenal gland or poor circulation. Depending on the severity of your condition, you may only need to apply a few of the suggestions below. For more information about each suggested product, visit **MarsVenus.com/supplements**. For more information about more energy and adrenal support, visit **MarsVenus.com/energy**.

1. Drink one cup of **Cho Wa** hot tea before or after breakfast, and after lunch. This is an old Japanese formula of 10 bitter herbs to stimulate and heal the adrenal glands. It only includes a tiny amount of caffeine from green tea extract. It supports adrenal health and also improves absorption of glucose. It is a great coffee replacement in the morning for those wishing to heal the adrenals.

2. Follow suggestions for Blood Sugar Issues. Fluctuating blood sugar levels exhaust your adrenals so they cannot heal.

3. Take one tablet of **Neo40** twice daily. Neo40 is made from red beets and increases circulation to bring oxygen to cells.

4. Take one capsule of **Adrenasense** twice daily.

5. Take one tablet of **DMG** twice daily. DMG is an amino acid taken to increase oxygenation of blood cells for extra energy.

6. Take one capsule of **ImmPower** twice daily. Fatigue can come from a chronic viral infection. This combination of special mushrooms are known to help combined with regular HT Therapy.

7. To restore adrenal function, take these four supplements twice daily for three months:
   - One half teaspoon of **Liposomal Vitamin C**
   - One capsule of **MSM**
   - One capsule of **Taurine**
   - One capsule of **Squalene**
8. Double the dosage in the second week. Then double that dosage in the third week and sustain this dosage for the rest of the three months.
9. Take six drops of **Goleic** once or twice a week. This is a much more powerful but expensive treatment. It can be ordered online at http://www.GCMAF.eu.

I only recommend **Goleic** last because it is much more expensive than other suggestions. If your budget allows, then this along with other suggested supplements would be a good first pick. It is a new program to restore your immune system by replacing a particular beneficial bacterium called GcMAF that is no longer being produced in the body.

It only takes three weeks to repopulate the gut but may take longer to fully heal. It has been used effectively to strengthen the immune system to help Chronic Fatigue Syndrome, autism and, in the first week of use, it has repeatedly proven to reduce cancer tumors by 25%. This is not a drug but an important probiotic that assists the immune system to fight viruses in the body.

Increased Muscle Mass

Both high muscle mass or low muscle mass can inhibit brain performance. When the muscles are not nutritionally supported, they tend to rob the brain of the amino acids needed to make brain chemicals. This is one of the reasons boys are so much more vulnerable to ADHD and autism. Boys, in general, have 30% more muscle mass than girls. In addition, girls have more estrogen which increases blood flow to the brain and has been shown to protect isolated neurons in the brain from oxidative stress.

A severe loss of muscle tone can also inhibit energy production. Without sufficient energy the brain is unable to heal. For increasing muscle mass any or all of these supplements added to your morning super food shake coupled with exercise will help. For more information about each suggested product, visit **MarsVenus.com/supplements**. For more information about increasing muscle mass for improved brain performance, visit **MarsVenus.com/muscle-mass.**

1. Add two scoops of **Collagen Peptides** to a **Super Foods Shake**.
2. Add one teaspoon of **Creatine Powder** to the **Super Foods Shake** or as indicated on the container.
3. Add two tablespoons of **MCT Oil** from coconut to the **Super Foods Shake**. Note: Gradually increase MCT Oil to the maximum dose of two tablespoons. Decrease dose if bloating or pain occurs due to candida die-off. Then gradually increase again.
4. Take one capsule of **PQQ** twice daily. This essential nutrient activates genes that promote the formation of new mitochondria (energy factories in muscle mass). It has also been shown to promote memory, attention and cognition in maturing individuals.

5. Take one capsule of **Tongkat Ali** twice daily. This natural herb stimulates your body to make more testosterone. For three months, each week, take for five days and then skip two days.

Digestion and Food Sensitivities

For improved digestion and food sensitivities, any or all of these supplements may help. To support brain function, digestion of proteins, fats and carbohydrates is essential. Depending on the severity of your condition, you may only need to apply a few of the suggestions below. You may also combine these suggestions with the Heavy Metal Detox diet listed above. For more information about each suggested product, visit **MarsVenus.com/products**. For more information about digestion and food sensitivities, visit **MarsVenus.com/digestion**.

1. Make a special Lemon Cleanse Drink and take 20 minutes before each meal or meal replacement shake. Mix together the following ingredients:
   - One teaspoon of **Mars Venus Super Cleanse**
   - One teaspoon of **Probiotics**
   - One scoop of **Collagen Peptides**
   - One scoop of **Acetyl-L-Carnitine**
   - One teaspoon of **MCT Oil**. Gradually increase MCT Oil to a maximum of one tablespoon. Decrease the amount if bloating or pain occurs due to candida die-off. Then gradually increase again.
2. Take two capsules of **Digestive Enzymes** 20 minutes before each meal or meal replacement shake.
3. Take one capsule of **Aloe Vera Polymannose Complex** before each meal or meal replacement shake to help heal the gut and strengthen cell membranes.
4. Take one capsule of **Resveratrol** 20 minutes before meals or meal replacement shake to help heal food allergies.
5. Take one capsule of **4-Constipation** before bed every night.
6. Temporarily go off pasteurized milk products, soy, corn, bread and other gluten products, sugar and other simple

carbohydrates, as well as packaged foods with preservative and food coloring. Simply eat real foods like meat, chicken, fish, vegetables, salads, and fruit. As symptoms are healed after weeks or several months, gradually reintroduce one food category at a time and wait a couple of days to see if symptoms return. After testing all food categories this way, wait a few months to test if you can reintroduce the food. Sometimes food allergies are healed this way and you can reintroduce offending foods.

Irritable Bowel Syndrome and Candida Control

Inflammation in the gut is always associated with inflammation in the brain. Irritable bowel syndrome includes symptoms of chronic abdominal pain, discomfort, bloating and diarrhea or constipation. This is usually accompanied by an overgrowth of candida in the gut. Any or all of the suggested products may help irritable bowel syndrome and control candida. Depending on the severity of your condition, you may only need to apply a few of the suggestions below. For more information about each suggested product, visit **MarsVenus.com/supplements**. For more information about irritable bowel syndrome and candida control, visit **MarsVenus.com/candida**.

1. Follow all of the guidelines and suggested supplements for Digestion and Food Sensitivities.

2. Take one **2-AEP Membrane Support** 20 minutes before every meal or meal replacement shake.

3. Take one teaspoon of **Colloidal Silver** first thing in the morning at least ten minutes before other supplements, in the afternoon on an empty stomach and before bed. Six half-droppers equals one teaspoon.

4. Follow the homeopathic protocol suggested by Dr. Salar for gastritis, worms and parasites. This can be purchased at **http://www.homeopathicwonders.com**.

5. Take six drops of **Goleic** once or twice a week before bed. Hold in mouth for 90 seconds. Do not drink fluids for one and half hours after taking. This is a much more powerful but expensive treatment. Take twice a week if you can afford the cost. It can be ordered online at **http://www.GCMAF.eu**.

I only recommend **Goleic** last because it is much more expensive than other suggestions. If your budget allows, then this along with other suggested supplements would be a good first pick. It is a new program to restore your immune system by replacing a particular beneficial bacterium called GcMAF that is no longer being produced in the body.

It only takes three weeks to repopulate the gut but may take longer to fully heal. It has been used effectively to strengthen the immune system to help Chronic Fatigue Syndrome, autism and, in the first week of use, it has repeatedly proven to reduce cancer tumors by 25%. This is not a drug but an important probiotic that assists the immune system to fight viruses in the body.

Strong Bones, Thicker Hair and Less Wrinkles

Efficient calcium absorption helps promote strong bones, thicker hair, reduced wrinkles and it is also required for your memory. For bone health, thicker hair and less wrinkles, any or all of the following supplements may help. For more information about each suggested product, visit **MarsVenus.com/supplements**. For more information about strong bones, thicker hair and less wrinkles, visit **MarsVenus.com/bones**.

1. Take one capsule of **Biosil** twice daily. This has proven to be more effective than drugs for strong bones and it has no side effects.
2. Take two **Super Minerals** twice daily.
3. If indicated by your other symptoms, follow suggestions for Blood Sugar Issues, Women's Hormone Balance or Irritable Bowel Syndrome. High blood sugar depletes the bones of calcium. Hormone imbalance of progesterone and estrogen weakens bones. Irritable bowel is linked to vitamin D deficiency, which inhibits calcium absorption in the bones.

Women's Hormone Balance

Hormone balance is essential for supporting memory and focus. For supporting healthy hormone balance in women, any or all of these suggestions and supplements may help. They are particularly good for PMS, hot flashes and a good night's sleep. Hot flashes result from low estrogen levels in the brain. Low estrogen is linked to a slowdown in the speed of brain processing, memory loss, insomnia and depression. Rather than replace hormones, these suggestions support healing your body to make its own healthy hormones. Depending on the severity of your condition, you may only need to apply a few of the suggestions below. For more information on relationship skills to stimulate healthy hormones read my book, *Venus On Fire, Mars On Ice*. For more information about each suggested product, visit **MarsVenus.com/supplements**. For more information about women's hormone balance, visit **MarsVenus.com/women-hormones**.

1. Take one capsule of **Mars Venus RX-W** 10 to 20 minutes before meals for as long as needed. This supplement contains three traditional Korean herbs proven to stop hot flashes and reduce PMS symptoms for many women and balancing hormone production.
2. Add one tablespoon of **Maca Powder** to the Super Foods Shake or a glass of diluted apple juice. My wife loves this one and it stopped her hot flashes.
3. Take one capsule of **Vitex** for increased production of progesterone and one capsule of **5-HTP** twice daily.
4. Take one capsule of **Hormone Balance** 10 to 20 minutes before each meal. This all-natural supplement contains extracts from flax, fruits and tubers designed to assist the body in making it's own hormones.

5. Optional three-month healing program: Take two capsules of **Myomin** before meals or meal replacement shakes. Myomin contains three Chinese herbs to assist detoxifying the liver of hormone disruptors to support hormone production.

6. Learn new communication and behavior skills for lowering stress and visit **MarsVenus.com/Collide-book**.

Women's Libido

Fulfilling romance and sex can directly lower a woman's stress levels and reduce oxidative stress in the brain. For increasing a woman's libido, any or all of these supplements may help. For more information about each suggested product, visit **MarsVenus.com/supplements**. For more information about women's libido, visit **MarsVenus.com/female-libido**.

1. Follow the instructions above for Women's Hormone Balance.

2. Take two capsules of **Lithium Orotate** twice daily. Low dose, lithium orotate is the most powerful natural stimulator of oxytocin. Oxytocin lowers a woman's stress levels and increases her sexual response.

3. For increased pleasure and interest in sex use an **herbal lubricant** to restore vaginal health. Due to stress and hormonal imbalance, as a woman ages, pleasure during sex may decrease as her vaginal walls become thinner. Regular application at night for three weeks can restore vaginal health.

4. For increased responsiveness and pleasure, take one capsule of **Brain Sharpener** two hours before having sex.

5. For increased responsiveness and interest, take one capsule of **Optimized Saffron** daily before meals and 2-4 capsules two hours before sex.

6. One half lozenge of **Neo 40** twice daily to improve blood flow to the genitals and one whole lozenge two hours before sex.

7. Take one capsule of **Tongkat Ali** daily and one extra capsule an hour before sex. Tongkat Ali helps to boost testosterone levels which for women can increase their interest in sex.

Natural Testosterone Boosters for Men

For men's hormone balance, any or all of these natural testosterone boosters may help. Lowering estrogen levels and boosting dopamine and testosterone levels can make a man feel younger again as well as reduce belly fat. Healthy dopamine and testosterone levels are essential to recharging a man's brainpower. Depending on the severity of your condition, you may only need to apply a few of the suggestions below. For more information about each suggested product, visit **MarsVenus.com/supplements**. For more information about the benefits of natural testosterone boosters for men, visit **MarsVenus.com/testosterone**.

1. Take two or three capsules of **Tongkat Ali** daily. This natural herb stimulates your body to make more testosterone. For three months, each week, take for five days and then skip two days.

2. Take two or three capsules of **Myomin,** 10-20 minutes before meals or meal replacement shakes for three months to reduce estrogen levels. Estrogen causes fat to be stored in the belly. When Myomin is combined with exercise, many men over 40 report a decrease in belly fat and improved prostate function.

3. Add one tablespoon of **Maca Powder** to the **Super Foods Shake**.

4. Take one **Brain Sharpener** daily, 10-20 minutes before meals or meal replacement shakes.

5. Take one **Hormone Balance** daily, 10-20 minutes before meals or meal replacement shakes.

6. Take one **4-Endocrine** daily, 10-20 minutes before meals or meal replacement shakes.

7. For long term overall anti-aging and hormone balance, take two capsules of **Product B** twice daily.

Men's Libido and Stamina

Regular sex is one of best ways to sustain youthful brain function. For men's libido, stamina and solid erections without the need for drugs like Viagra or Cialis, any or all of these supplements may help. Depending on the severity of your condition, you may only need to apply a few of the suggestions below. For more information about each suggested product, visit **MarsVenus.com/supplements**. For more information about increasing a man's interest in sex as well as increasing stamina in sex, visit **MarsVenus.com/mens-libido**.

1. Follow the suggestions in Appendix One and the suggestions for Natural Testosterone Boosters.
2. Take one capsule of **Brain Sharpener** one or two hours before sex.
3. Take two capsules of **Vitex** one or two hours before sex. Vitex is greatly misunderstood. It has the effect of lessening ones interest in addictive sex and porn but increases interest in having personal and intimate sex.
4. Take two capsules of **Tongkat Ali** one or two hours before sex.
5. Take one lozenge of **Neo 40** once or twice daily. Neo 40 is a natural extract from red beets that increases nitric oxide production to increase circulation to the genitals.
6. To occasionally last longer during intercourse, follow the suggestions above and take two to four capsules of **Gabatrol** four hours before sex. For some people, Gabatrol may make you sleepy so it needs to be combined with a cup of tea or coffee. For more suggestions go to **MarsVenus.com/extend**.

A Good Night's Sleep

Less than seven hours of sleep has been shown in studies to impair memory by 30%. Sleep is the ultimate hormone producer. Chronic disturbances in sleep can interfere with both brain healing and balanced blood sugar. The following suggestions can help insure a good night's sleep almost every night.

1. 1. Exercise or go for a walk first thing in the morning after drinking the Lemon Cleanse Drink and two **Super Minerals.**
   Mix together the following ingredients:
   - One teaspoon of **Mars Venus Super Cleanse**
   - One teaspoon of **Probiotics**
   - One scoop of **Collagen Peptides**
   - One scoop of **Acetyl-L-Carnitine**
   - One teaspoon of **MCT Oil.** Gradually increase MCT Oil to a maximum of one tablespoon. Decrease the amount if bloating or pain occurs due to candida die-off. Then gradually increase again.

2. If you are waking up in the night and can't get back to sleep, this may be due to a sudden drop in blood sugar, which in turn spikes cortisol. Follow the instructions previously listed for balancing blood sugar.

3. If you are getting up in the night to use the bathroom, take two to four capsules of **Flower Pollen** a few hours before sleep. Try to minimize drinking water two hours before going to sleep.

4. A forty minute bath with one or two cups of Epson salts and low lights before bed will make all the difference until you set up a healthy routine or habit of falling asleep for

at least 7 hours of uninterrupted sleep. To prevent boredom, listen to a recorded book.

5. For men, **Prostate Plus** contains natural ingredients known to increase urine flow as well as prevent the need to use the bathroom during your sleep time.

6. Rotate the use of **Tranquil Sleep** and **Muscle Relax** to set up a good habit of going to bed and waking up at the same time every day. Each of these supplements works in different ways. By alternating them you can prevent your brain from becoming dependent on one. Set your goal to not depend on them but to use them to create the habit of sleeping through the night. Then keep them around to use when you are traveling and have to deal with falling asleep in a different time zone or on a long flight. The less you use them, the better they work when you really need them.

Freedom from Drugs and Sickness

For a more in depth understanding of the many benefits of natural supplements go to **MarsVenus.com/health-blogs**. There are free video health blogs exploring natural solutions for a wide range of condition from allergies and headaches to colds to constipation. With greater insight, you can minimize or even eliminate the need for prescription and over-the-counter drugs. With this knowledge, you can access your power to choose a lifetime of health, happiness and love.

Appendix Four

Suggested Behaviors To Recharge Your Brainpower

Recharging your brainpower demands that you stop producing oxidative stress in your brain. In Chapter Four, we discussed the many ways you may be causing oxidative stress. The next step is to reset the brain while it has a chance to heal. Good nutrition and supplements are required but we also need certain types of positive stimulation to fully utilize the good nutrition.

Once the brain is reset, then it becomes easy to release old limiting habits, patterns and addictions and replace them with new more supportive patterns of thinking, feeling and acting. We will explore this next step in the process of transformation in Book Two of *Staying Focused In A Hyper World*. But for now, to first reset the brain, we need good nutrition and positive mental, emotional, sensory and physical stimulation.

Mental stimulation: Practice some form of meditation or prayer on a regular basis. Regular meditation or prayer is an opportunity to strengthen your ability to effortlessly direct your attention according to your will rather than becoming restless, distracted, overwhelmed or over-reactive. With practice, due to brain plasticity, you are literally increasing the neural connections in your brain between the prefrontal cortex (will) and the limbic system (automatic reactions.) With this increased neural connection, along with the right nutritional support, you can heal the injury in the nucleus accumbens caused by oxidative stress and restore access to your full mental potential.

In Book Two of *Staying Focused In A Hyper World*, we will explore a range of meditative techniques to increase brain performance according to your unique temperament. Some people have difficulty meditating because they assume they must close their eyes and sit still. There are different forms of meditation for your unique temperament that do not involve sitting still.

In the meantime, a powerful meditation practice can be just setting aside five to ten minutes before bed to reflect on what you did that day, what you learned, and what you are grateful for. In addition, another helpful meditation is simply taking a few minutes in the morning to review what you plan to do, how you want to feel and what you are grateful for.

For children, a set routine of reading positive and uplifting books can help. Even better, to improve sleep and behavior, give children a 30-40 minute Epson salt bath. Increase the water temperature after 10 minutes from 101 to 103 degrees Fahrenheit. Read them stories, sing songs or read prayers at night. A little hydrothermal therapy as discussed in Chapter Twelve can help everyone and not just children with autism.

Reading before bed is also helpful for adults. You determine your destiny by the people you surround yourself with and sleep with. Even by reading or listening to positive and inspiring books, you are connecting with those authors and getting the benefit of their company. Take a course or class in something that interests you so that you are learning something new along with others. Join me or my daughter, Lauren Gray, every day at **MarsVenus.com**. We make uplifting video blogs for creating a lifetime of love, happiness and health. If you need answers to your particular relationship challenges, sign up for an Email Advice Package at **MarsVenus. com/lauren.**

Emotional Stimulation: Make sure you surround yourself with friends and people who care about you. Set up a regular routine at least once or twice a month to participate in a support group of some kind to share with like-minded people to grow in mutual friendship. Make sure all your friends are not only digital friends online. Practice journaling your emotional experiences. Make a gratitude journal or practice the love letter technique as described in my book *What You Feel You Can Heal.*

If you are going through a stressful or difficult time, talk with a coach or counselor to share the thoughts and feelings that may be difficult to share with your friends. Take transformational seminars and workshops. Join me at one of my **Soul Mate Seminars** in California. Talk to a Mars Venus Life Coach or talk on the telephone to a Mars Venus Relationship Coach. For more information on seminars and coaching, visit **MarsVenus.com/ seminars** and **MarsVenus.com/coaching**.

Sensory Stimulation: Make sure to listen to uplifting music every day. Feel the warmth of the sun on your skin as much as possible. Direct sunshine produces Vitamin D, which in turn reduces oxidative stress. If you get burned easily, then take **astaxanthin** capsules and you will not burn with moderate sun exposure (20 to 40 minutes).

Get a regular massage or if you have a willing partner have regular sex at least once a week. These activities and lots of hugs are major oxytocin producers to help lower stress, particularly for women. For men, sex is a bit more important because it also stimulates both dopamine and testosterone. Testosterone is the key hormone for lowering stress in men.

If you are not drawn to sensory pleasing touch or sensation, taking lithium orotate or pine nut oil will jump-start your ability to enjoy touch, just as taking astaxanthin increases your ability to enjoy the pleasure of the sun bathing. In a similar way, taking **Tongkat Ali** increases testosterone levels, which in turn increases your ability to enjoy sex and regular exercise.

As I have already mentioned, Internet porn and impersonal sex increase oxidative stress and ADHD, while sex with a partner you know and love creates a different set of hormones that reduces oxidative stress in the brain. Impersonal sex spikes dopamine, testosterone and decreases prolactin levels similar to taking heroin while personal sex increases oxytocin, increases prolactin levels and allows one to fully relax, decreasing oxidative stress.

Take time to enjoy your foods and make sure to spend time in nature at least twice a week. Healthy sensory stimulation leaves you satisfied while over stimulation leaves you wanting more. Plan activities that will stimulate you with at least one new experience every week. For couples this can be a date night.

Physical Stimulation: Exercise, exercise and exercise is necessary for healthy brain function and longevity. A minimum of thirty minutes, three times a week is required. Physical movement is the foundation for brain health. More is even better. Yet, many people who do exercise don't get the full benefit of exercise because they don't take the time to rest and relax afterwards. This recovery period is just as important as the exercise.

**The recovery period after exercise
is just as important as the exercise.**

Intermittent exercise is the best exercise to reduce oxidative stress. For best results, follow these simple instructions.

1. Walk or exercise for two to five minutes.
2. Then for twenty seconds increase the intensity of exercise to the max without hurting yourself.
3. Then relax and allow yourself to be out of breath. You can simply sit down and relax or adjust your exercise to a very low intensity for two to four minutes. During this time, avoid the temptation to take a deep inhale which stops you from being out of breath.
4. That's all there is to it. This is one cycle. For best results do a total of two to six cycles.

**After exercise, avoid the temptation
to take a deep inhale
which stops you from being out of breath.**

During the two to four minute recovery period, allow the state of being out of breath to naturally return to normal breath. I call this state of being out of breath and gradually returning to normal breath your "recovery breath."

As long as your exhale is automatically longer than your inhale, you are experiencing your body's natural recovery breath; at this time your body is reducing oxidative stress and producing repair enzymes vital for your brain health and vitality.

When the exhaled breath gradually becomes shorter and equal to the inhaled breath, it is time to resume your exercise once again for two to five minutes. Then push yourself to the max for twenty seconds. Then relax and experience your recovery breath for two to four minutes. This recovery breath needs to be automatic. In the beginning, it may only be two minutes and that is still helpful. As you learn to fully relax your mind and body while experiencing the automatic recovery breath, it will eventually extend to four minutes.

Being out of breath is the most important part of exercise. Over time, gradually increase to six cycles. Intermittent exercise should only be done twice a week for maximum results. Even once a week will have profound benefits. In addition, normal exercise or walking for extended periods of times is recommended.

**Being out of breath
is the most important part of exercise.**

Sometimes we need extra help to break out of our sedentary habits. If you are not exercising, then get a coach or a walking buddy who will inspire you to exercise. Or even get a dog so that you have to go for a walk every day. For extra fun, check out my Isoflex Exercise Video at **MarsVenus.com/Isoflex**. It focuses on easy exercises for brain health, hormone balance and increasing strength.

If you have had a lifetime of ADHD or if your symptoms are severe, then learning the brain stimulating movements developed by Anat Baniel may dramatically help to reset your brain in a much shorter period of time. For more information about the Anat Baniel Method go to http://www.anatbanielmethod.com.

Appendix Five

Official Disclaimer

As with any book regarding heath, the authors are required to remind you that their ideas or the studies they quote are for your information only and not intended to diagnose, prevent or cure any disease you may have. The information in this book is to educate you so that you can make your own conclusions or decisions regarding your health and happiness.

Besides being a relationship expert for the last forty years, I am a writer and researcher and have taught popular and professional seminars on health for over twelve years. Any suggestions that I make are my opinion only and are based on my personal experience. This book is designed to give you an alternative perspective for your health particularly when it comes to non-drug solutions for mental performance, memory and the brain condition commonly expressed and identified as ADHD.

Any radical changes you make to your diet or exercise regime should be reviewed by your health care provider or trusted health advocate. I have done my best to provide easy solutions that anyone can apply to feel happier, healthier and more focused.

This, however, presents a new challenge. When taking certain drugs it is not always safe to become healthier. If you are taking a blood thinner and you became healthier, then it would be unsafe to continue taking the same dose of your blood thinner. The blood thinner works for thick blood to become thinner, but it will also make healthy blood too thin, which is dangerous to your health. In this case, the choice is yours. Do you want to be healthier and live a long healthy life or stay sick and continue depending on drugs with all their known side effects?

**When you are taking some drugs,
it is not safe to become healthier.**

The same is true for diabetics who take insulin. If you become healthier, it could be dangerous to continue taking the same amount of insulin. Insulin, which lowers blood sugar levels, is only safe to take if you have unhealthy high blood sugar levels. If your blood sugar levels become healthy again, then taking insulin would make them drop too low. With natural solutions, as you find your way back to healthy blood sugar levels, it is important that you closely monitor your blood sugar levels to gradually lower your dose of insulin.

A major part of healing the brain and preventing memory loss is balancing blood sugar without the need for insulin. Most people today are surprised to hear that the number one risk factor for dementia and Alzheimer's disease is high blood sugar levels, whether you have diabetes or not. Researchers are now calling Alzheimer's disease "diabetes of the brain." To achieve optimal brain performance and overcome the challenges of memory loss and ADHD, gradually giving up the need for drugs is essential.

**The number one risk factor for dementia
and Alzheimer's disease is high blood sugar levels.**

While blood thinners and insulin are dangerous if you become healthier; the other prescription drugs, to different degrees, interfere with your brain's ability to heal. For example, if you are taking Lipitor, or any other statin drug for lowering cholesterol, your chance of dementia or Alzheimer's increases.

A variety of studies have discovered that high cholesterol levels are necessary for long life and healthy brain function. And yet, Lipitor is still the bestselling drug in the history of pharmaceuticals. During the writing of this book, after 14 years of ignoring reports of memory loss and confusion from the use of Lipitor, the FDA expanded their advice on the risks. The FDA is finally advising consumers and health care professionals "that cognitive impairment, such as memory loss, forgetfulness and confusion, has been reported by some statin users." In addition, "people being treated with statins may have increased risk of raised blood sugar levels and the development of Type 2 diabetes."

After 14 years, the FDA admits
Lipitor may cause cognitive impairment.

The natural solutions presented in this book can help you to heal the body and brain. Drugs do not and cannot heal. They can only suppress symptoms while producing unwanted side effects. Drugs can, however, give you more time to find natural solutions that will work for you.

If you are already drug-free in your search for optimal brain performance, the natural solutions will work more quickly. They can also work as you gradually reduce your drug use. It just takes longer.

The process of decreasing your drug use is a question for your drug provider. For each person, according to his or her background, the protocol may be different. Your health care provider should know the seriousness of decreasing the use of a particular drug.

In approaching your provider, don't be surprised if they are a bit resistant to reducing the use of your drugs. Certainly they want to help but they believe they are already giving you the best solution. In most cases, if your doctor already understood natural solutions, then they would have suggested them.

The ideas in this book are new and cutting-edge, so most doctors have not yet heard of them. In approaching your doctor with changes you want to make, avoid asking for permission, but instead share your intention to use a natural solution and then ask what protocol they would suggest in going off the medications you are taking.

Most of the ideas in this book are new and cutting-edge, so most doctors have not yet heard of them.

If you ask doctors for permission, most are legally liable and can be sued if they don't follow their standard drug protocols. In some hospitals, doctors can lose their license or job for recommending alternative, natural, drug-free solutions. Even if they felt legally free to give their own advice, it would be irresponsible to suggest anything "new" that they have not worked with or have any updated knowledge of.

Doctors can lose their license or job for recommending natural, drug-free solutions.

Doctors may not know about the new solutions but they do know the problems you may encounter going off a drug. Suddenly stopping a particular drug can sometimes be more dangerous than continuing to take the drug. Reducing your drug use may take weeks to many months, depending upon your condition and how long you have been taking the drugs.

Unlike conventional doctors, most "complementary doctors," who have also studied nutrition and other forms of healing, will be happy to hear that you are taking responsibility for your brain and body with extra nutrition. In most cases, they will suggest gradually reducing the use of drugs as your health improves.

To the best of my knowledge, every recommendation I explore in this book, unless noted, is completely compatible with any drug you may be taking except blood thinners and insulin. In the process of getting healthier, you need to carefully monitor the appropriate use of these drugs.

Discussing new ideas to improve your health with conventional doctors is your choice but keep in mind new natural solutions are not a part of their training. Their standard advice is to say "eat a good diet and get regular exercise." This is certainly good advice but it is not enough.

It is not enough to say,
"Eat a good diet and get regular exercise."

Keep in mind that just because your doctor is not aware of a natural, drug-free solution, it doesn't mean it will not work. There may not be a double-blind study to validate every natural protocol but that does not mean they are ineffective. There are now hundreds of studies showing the benefits of natural supplements to improve memory and heal ADHD while also improving brain performance at any age. Double-blind studies are not always necessary to validate a treatment. For example, there have been no double-blind studies on heart surgeries and yet they save lives every day. And there are no double-blind studies on the benefits or side effects from combining four or five different drugs, which is commonly done everyday.

There are no double-blind studies
that validate heart surgery.

Throughout this book, we have refrained from using the word "cure" and instead used the word "heal." This is actually more appropriate because a "cure" implies that a condition will never come back. Using the term "healing" is more accurate because once the condition that creates "dis-ease" in the brain or body is corrected or "healed," it may be recreated at any time, if we do not stop the very things that caused the condition in the first place.

Appendix Six

Notes and References

Preface

1. "Did you know that one out of ten American children have been diagnosed with ADHD?"

A. Reference from Associated Press quoting the Center For Disease Control in 2011 printed in USA Today, November 22, 2013.

"More than half of these children are diagnosed (with ADHD) by 6 years old. ADHD has been increasing every year. Nearly one in every five high school-age boys has received a medical diagnosis of ADHD. 11% of school-age children have been diagnosed."

B. http://www.usatoday.com/story/news/nation/2013/11/22/adhd-kids-cdc/3677883/.

C. http://www.nytimes.com/2013/04/01/health/more-diagnoses-of-hyperactivity-causing-concern.html?pagewanted=all&_r=0

D. http://www.webmd.com/add-adhd/childhood-adhd/news/20101109/cdc-nearly-1-10-kids-has-adhd

2. Did you know that one out of nine students in America today seriously contemplate suicide every year?

Reference from NBC news: "Half of college students consider suicide" http://www.nbcnews.com/id/26272639/ns/health-mental_health/t/half-college-students-consider-suicide/#.U1qcEZG4rRo

"The study extrapolated that at an average college with 18,000 undergraduate students, 1,080 of them would seriously contemplate taking their lives in any year, numbers that pose troubling issues for college administrators."

3. "Did you know that one out of eight American teenagers suffer from depression?"

Reference from ABC news: "Teen Sadness May Be Depression" Andrew Colton, May 2

http://abcnews.go.com/Health/story?id=117478

"One out of every eight teens suffers from depression, a condition so serious it leads 5,000 teens in the United States to commit suicide each year."

4. "Did you know that one out of seven American women over 55 will develop dementia?"

Reference from Institute for Dementia Research & Prevention: "FAQ"

http://idrp.pbrc.edu/faq.htm

"In the US there are believed to be at least 5 million individuals with age-related dementias. In Louisiana there are at least 100,000 individuals with age-related dementia. These numbers will only to continue to rise with the aging of the US population. It is estimated that 1 in 6 women, and 1 in 10 men, who live past the age of 55 will develop dementia in their lifetime."

5. "Did you know that one out of six American children have a developmental disability?"

Reference from CDC: Autism Spectrum Disorder

http://www.cdc.gov/ncbddd/autism/data.html

"About 1 in 6 children in the United States had a developmental disability in 2006-2008, ranging from mild disabilities such as speech and language impairments to serious developmental disabilities, such as intellectual disabilities, cerebral palsy, and autism"

6. Did you know that one out of five Americans suffer from a mental disorder in a given year?

Reference by The Science of Mental Illness and the Brain

http://science.education.nih.gov/supplements/nih5/mental/guide/info-mental-a.htm

"According to recent estimates, approximately 20 percent of Americans, or about one in five people over the age of 18, suffer from a diagnosable mental disorder in a given year."

"About 5 percent of adults are affected so seriously by mental illness that it interferes with their ability to function in society. These severe and persistent mental illnesses include schizophrenia, bipolar, depression, panic disorder, and obsessive-compulsive disorder."

7. Did you know that one out of four children in America have been bullied or attacked?

Reference from Bullying Statistics: "2009"

http://www.bullyingstatistics.org/content/bullying-statistics-2009.html

8. "Did you know that one out of three adults over seventy suffer significant memory loss?"

Reference from Duke University Medical Center: "How common is memory Loss?" Sharon O'Brien

http://seniorliving.about.com/od/alzheimersdementia1/a/memory_impairme.htm

"If you're over age 70 and have occasional memory lapses, you're not alone. More than a third of people over age 70 have some form of memory loss, according to a national study.

Researchers at Duke University Medical Center, the University of Michigan, the University of Iowa, the University of Southern California and the RAND Corporation report that while an estimated 3.4 million Americans have dementia, which they define as a loss of the ability to function independently, an additional 5.4 million people over age 70 have memory loss that "disrupts their regular routine but is not severe enough to affect their ability to complete daily activities."

9. "Did you know that one out of two adults over 85 have Alzheimer's disease?"

Reference from Alzheimer's Association: "Did You Know?"
http://www.alz.org/documents/nwohio/alzheimers_facts_figures.pdf

"One out of eight people age 65 and older has Alzheimer's Disease and nearly one out of two people over the age 85 have the disease or a related disorder."

10. "Did you know that one out of 42 boys is diagnosed with autism?"

Reference from CDC: Autism Spectrum Disorder
http://www.cdc.gov/ncbddd/autism/data.html

"ASD is almost 5 times more common among boys (1 in 42) than among girls (1 in 189)"

11. "Did you know all of these statistics are increasing every year?"

A. Reference from CDC: "Mental Health Surveillance Among Children"

"This study reported a 24% increase in inpatient mental health and substance abuse admissions among children during 2007-2010."

B. Reference from Alzheimer's Society: "Demography" http://www.alzheimers.org.uk/site/scripts/documents_info. php?documentID=412

"The number of people with dementia is steadily increasing."

C. Reference from CDC: "ADHD Estimates Rise" http://www.cdc.gov/media/dpk/2013/dpk-ADHD-esti-mates-rise.html

"Two million more children in the United States have been diagnosed with attention-deficit/hyperactivity disorder (ADHD) and one million more U.S. children were taking medication for ADHD over an 8 year period (2003-2004 to 2011-2012), according to a new study."

12. "Mental illness is thirty-five times more common today than thirty years ago."

Reference by Robert Whitaker author of *Anatomy Of An Epidemic,* an in depth look at the rise of mental illness in America. http://robertwhitaker.org/robertwhitaker.org/Anatomy%20 of%20an%20Epidemic.html

"In 1955, there were 355,000 adults in state and county mental hospitals with a psychiatric diagnosis. During the next three decades (the era of the first generation psychiatric drugs), the number of disabled mentally ill rose to 1.25 million. Prozac arrived on the market in 1988, and during the next 20 years, the number of disabled mentally ill grew to more than four million adults (in 2007.) Finally, the prescribing of psychiatric medications to children and adolescents took off during this period (1987 to 2007), and as this medical practice took hold, the number of youth in America receiving a government disability check because of a mental illness leapt from 16,200 in 1987 to 561,569 in 2007 (a 35-fold increase.)"

13. "More than half of these children are diagnosed before 6 years old."

Reference from The Journal of the American Academy of Child and Adolescent Psychiatry: "Continued Increases in ADHD Diagnoses and Treatment With Medication Among U.S. Children" http://www.jaacap.com/webfiles/images/journals/jaac/jaac_pr_53_1_1.pdf

"New study led by the CDC reports that half of U.S. children diagnosed with ADHD received that diagnosis by age 6."

"According to CDC scientists, children are commonly being diagnosed at a young age. Parents report that half of children diagnosed with ADHD were diagnosed by 6 years of age, but children with more severe ADHD tended to be diagnosed earlier, about half of them by the age of 4.

Introduction

1. "Since that time, studies have been carried out on many of the same ingredients. These studies have proven that specific natural supplements can heal the brain."

A. Reference from International Journal of General Medicine: "Amino acid management of Parkinson's disease: a case study." Marty Hinz and associates.

"Virtually all of the problems associated with Parkinson's disease and L-dopa are caused by the numerous relative nutritional deficiencies that are brought about by the disease or develop in the course of standard L-dopa treatment. These nutritional deficiencies and their management were only defined in recent years by the medical research project of Marty Hinz, MD. Addressing these nutritional deficiencies properly achieves optimal results and stops progression of the disease in its tracks."

B. Reference from Alvin Stein, MD: "Parkinson's Disease"

http://www.neurosciencemyths.com/Parkinson's-disease.htm

"Even patients with severe Parkinson's disease can ultimately expect significant improvement with this approach. Patients can expect that their Parkinson's disease pills will not stop working during treatment, something that is currently a problem in conventional treatment. Patients can also expect to halt or drastically slow the progression of the disease."

2. "In the 1800's, while recovering from a devastating Civil War, America became a nation of drunkards. Men drank three times as much alcohol as we do now."

Reference from PBS special: Prohibition. http://www.pbs.org/kenburns/prohibition/about/episode-guide/

"… by 1830, the average American over fifteen years old consumes nearly seven gallons of pure alcohol a year, three times as much as we drink today. Alcohol abuse, mostly perpetrated by men, wreaks havoc on the lives of many families, and women, with few legal rights or protection, are utterly dependent on their husbands for sustenance and support. As a wave of spiritual fervor for reform sweeps the country, many women and men begin to see alcohol as a scourge, an impediment to a Protestant vision of clean and righteous living."

3. "It is estimated that one out five Americans suffers from a diagnosable mental disorder in a given year."

A. Reference by The Science of Mental Illness and the Brain

http://science.education.nih.gov/supplements/nih5/mental/guide/info-mental-a.htm

"Consider the following statistics to get an idea of just how widespread the effects of mental illness are in society:

1. According to recent estimates, approximately 20 percent of Americans, or about one in five people over the age of 18, suffer from a diagnosable mental disorder in a given year.

2. Four of the 10 leading causes of disability—major depression, bipolar disorder, schizophrenia, and obsessive-compulsive disorder—are mental illnesses.

3. About 3 percent of the population has more than one mental illness at a time.

4. About 5 percent of adults are affected so seriously by mental illness that it interferes with their ability to function in society. These severe and persistent mental illnesses include schizophrenia, bipolar disorder, depression, panic disorder, and obsessive-compulsive disorder.

5. Approximately 20 percent of doctors' appointments are related to anxiety disorders such as panic attacks.

6. Eight million people have depression each year.

7. Two million Americans have schizophrenia disorders, and 300,000 new cases are diagnosed each year."

B. Reference by ABC News: "One in Five Americans Suffers From Mental Illness" by Mikaela Conley Jan. 19, 2012

http://abcnews.go.com/blogs/health/2012/01/19/1-in-5-americans-suffer-from-mental-illness/

"One in five Americans experienced some sort of mental illness in 2010, according to a new report from the Substance Abuse and Mental Health Services Administration. About 5 percent of Americans have suffered from such severe mental illness that it interfered with day-to-day school, work or family."

"Women were more likely to be diagnosed with mental illness than men (23 percent of women versus 16.9 percent of men), and the rate of mental illness was more than twice as likely in young adults (18 to 25) than people older than 50."

4. "The outcome of using prescribed drugs to treat mental illness is a shocking increase of 35 times more mental illness in 30 years. "

Reference by Robert Whitaker author of *Anatomy Of An Epidemic,* an in depth look at the rise of mental illness in America. http://robertwhitaker.org/robertwhitaker.org/Anatomy%20 of%20an%20Epidemic.html

Hundreds of studies can be found in his book or website to back up his analysis of the shocking failure of prescribed drugs for mental illness and ADHD. For those who want all the technical specifics and history his book is an eye opening excellent read. Here is brief summary from his website:

"About the Book"

Anatomy of an Epidemic investigates a medical mystery: Why has the number of adults and children disabled by mental illness skyrocketed over the past fifty years? There are now more than four million people in the United States who receive a government disability check because of a mental illness, and the number continues to soar. Every day, 850 adults and 250 children with a mental illness are added to the government disability rolls. What is going on?

The Mystery

The modern era of psychiatry is usually said to have begun with the introduction of Thorazine into asylum medicine in 1955. This kicked off a "psychopharmacological revolution," or so our society is told, with psychiatry discovering effective drugs for mental disorders of all kinds. In 1988, the first of the "second-generation" psychiatric drugs, Prozac, was introduced, and these new drugs were said to represent another therapeutic advance. Yet, even as this "psychopharmacological revolution" has unfolded over the past 50 years, the number of people disabled by mental illness has soared.

In 1955, there were 355,000 adults in state and county mental hospitals with a psychiatric diagnosis. During the next three decades (the era of the first generation psychiatric drugs), the number of disabled mentally ill rose to 1.25 million. Prozac arrived on the market in 1988, and during the next 20 years, the number of disabled mentally ill grew to more than four million adults (in 2007.) Finally, the prescribing of psychiatric medications to children and adolescents took off during this period (1987 to 2007), and as this medical practice took hold, the number of youth in America receiving a government disability check because of a mental illness leapt from 16,200 in 1987 to 561,569 in 2007 (a 35-fold increase.)

The Investigation

The astonishing increase in the disability numbers during the past fifty years raises an obvious question: Could the widespread use of psychiatric medications, for one reason or another, be fueling this epidemic? *Anatomy of an Epidemic* investigates that question, and it does so by focusing on the long-term outcome studies in the research literature. Do the studies tell of a paradigm of care that helps people get well and stay well over the long-term? Or do they tell of a paradigm of care that increases the likelihood that people diagnosed with mental disorders will become chronically ill?

The Documents

This website is designed to provide readers of *Anatomy of an Epidemic* with access to the key studies reviewed in the book."

5. The fact that both identical twins in a pair don't develop the same disease 100% of the time indicates that other factors are involved.

Reference from Genetic Science Learning Center : "Insights From Identical Twins"

http://learn.genetics.utah.edu/content/epigenetics/twins/

"To illustrate, for twins with schizophrenia, 50% identical twins share the disease, while only about 10-15% of fraternal twins do. This difference is evidence for a strong genetic component in susceptibility to schizophrenia. However, the fact that both identical twins in a pair don't develop the disease 100% of the time indicates that other factors are involved."

Chapter One: Focus

1. "In epidemic proportions, more children at school are falling behind."

Reference by PBS, Bill Moyers on http://billmoyers.com/episode/full-show-neil-degrasse-tyson-on-science-literacy/

"...Our Secretary of Education, Arne Duncan, calls it "educational stagnation." Consider this, PISA tests, tests that measure critical thinking in science, math, and reading among high school students in different countries, show that our students aren't doing so well.

In math, students in 33 other countries, including Ireland, Poland, Latvia, the United Kingdom and the Czech Republic, did better than American students. In science, students in 24 countries including Poland, Ireland, and the Czech Republic were ahead of ours. And in reading, our best subject, kids in 21 countries outdid the Americans.

The hard truth, says Secretary Duncan, is that the United States is not among the top performing comparable countries in any subject tested by PISA. That's bad news for our students and the country."

2. "ADHD is now the most commonly studied and diagnosed psychiatric disorder in children and adolescents."

Reference from Wikipedia: ADHD
http://en.wikipedia.org/wiki/
Attention_deficit_hyperactivity_disorder

3. "Researchers have found that the brains of children with ADHD are actually different from children without ADHD."

A. Reference from the National Institute Of Mental Health: "Brain Changes Mirror Symptoms in ADHD"

http://www.nimh.nih.gov/news/science-news/2006/brain-changes-mirror-symptoms-in-adhd.shtml

"The severity of attention-deficit hyperactivity disorder (ADHD) symptoms in youth appears to be reflected in their brain structure, recent NIMH-supported brain imaging studies are finding. In one study, researchers found that the front part of the brain's memory hub, the hippocampus, tended to be enlarged in ADHD, particularly in children with fewer symptoms. They suggest that such changes might develop as a compensatory response that helps the child cope with the impatience and stimulus-seeking problems of the disorder."

"The researchers also found that parts of an emotion-processing hub, the amygdala, were smaller in children with the disorder. The diminished size had a significant and positive correlation with severity of ADHD symptoms. In those with the disorder, researchers also observed poor connections between the amygdala and the prefrontal cortex, which could contribute to problems with impulse control and goal-directed behaviors."

"... to study this, researchers scanned the brains of 163 children with ADHD and 166 healthy controls, averaging about 9 years old. They re-scanned about 60 percent of each group again about 5.7 years later."

"The ADHD group initially had a thinner cortex, most prominently in frontal areas that control attention and motor activity. These changes turned out to be much greater in patients who showed less improvement at follow-up, about six years later. In children with the best outcomes, an area of the cortex associated with attention (right parietal cortex) had increased thickness and resembled that of healthy peers by follow-up."

B. Reference from HealthDay News: "ADHD Brain Changes Appear to Persist Into Adulthood" Xavier Castellanos, M.D.,University of Pittsburgh School of Medicine, Pa.; November 2011, *Archives of General Psychiatry*

"http://www.medicinenet.com/script/main/art.asp? articlekey=151510

"Adults who were diagnosed with attention-deficit hyperactivity disorder (ADHD) as children have less gray matter in certain areas of their brains as adults than people who didn't have ADHD in their youth, researchers say.

"The majority of individuals with ADHD improve in adulthood, but it was still somewhat disappointing to see that even with improvement, there continue to be challenges for those with ADHD," said the study's lead author, Dr. F. Xavier Castellanos, a professor of child and adolescent psychiatry at New York University Langone Medical Center in New York City..."

4. "In addition, researchers at the Brookhaven National Laboratory have published a study showing that the use of stimulant drugs to treat ADHD changes the brain making the disorder even worse. Dopamine function in the brain is inhibited by 24%."

Reference from Play Attention: "Long-Term Use of ADHD Medications Changes Brain Function: What every parent and adult needs to know"

http://www.playattention.com/ long-term-adhd-medications-brain-function-2/

Based on report by: Researchers at Brookhaven National Laboratory http://www.plosone.org/article/info%3Adoi%2F10.1371%2Fjournal. pone.0063023

"For many years, dopamine, a neurotransmitter (a brain chemical that transmits a message from a brain cell to another brain cell), was thought to be primary culprit in ADHD. Dopamine plays a major function in the brain as it is responsible for reward-motivated behavior. A plethora of studies have shown rewards increase the level of dopamine in the brain. This is what makes us motivated to get rewarded. Many drugs, including cocaine, Ritalin, and methamphetamine, act by amplifying the effects of dopamine. Too little dopamine means greater distractibility and riskier behavior as the brain constantly seeks ways to increase its dopamine levels.

Researchers at Brookhaven National Laboratory published a study examining levels of dopamine in ADHD patients who had never taken stimulants. They reviewed dopamine transporter density. Transporters actually filter dopamine away from its receptors in the brain. More transporters means less dopamine (and therefore less bang for the reward). Transporter density was determined through PET brain scans.

Initial scans found no differences among their small population of 18 adults who suffered from ADHD but were never treated for it. This group was then treated with Ritalin. After a year, the researchers discovered that dopamine transporter density increased by 24 percent. What this study found was in fact what many parents have discovered during their child's use of medication; taking ADHD medication may change the brain's chemistry so that the effects of the medication are reduced over time. To accommodate this, one's pediatrician or medical doctor will often increase the dosage due to drug tolerance."

5. "Adults also can have ADHD; up to half of adults diagnosed with the disorder had it as children."

Reference from WebMD: "Attention-deficit Hyperactivity Disorder: Symptoms of ADHD"

http://www.webmd.com/add-adhd/guide/adhd-symptoms

Chapter Two: Natural Solutions for ADHD

1. "…stimulant drugs have certainly helped many millions of children but they also create undesirable short-term and long-term side effects."

A. Reference from New York Time: "ADHD." This article summarizes some of the good and bad long-term and short-term side effects by A.D.A.M.

http://www.nytimes.com/health/guides/disease/attention-deficit-hyperactivity-disorder-adhd/medications.html

B. Reference psychcentral.com. This article summarizes the long-term side effects of ADHD medications. By Jane Collingwood http://psychcentral.com/lib/side-effects-of-adhd-medications/0003782

2. "Even stimulant drug manufacturers admit these drugs have repeatedly failed to heal the condition."

Reference from the National Institute of Mental Health

http://www.nimh.nih.gov/health/publications/mental-health-medications/index.shtml?utm_source=rss_readers&utm_medium=rss&utm_campaign=rss_full

"Medications treat the symptoms of mental disorders. They cannot cure the disorder, but they make people feel better so they can function."

3. "In many American hospitals, cancer doctors can lose their jobs or even go to jail for recommending anything other than chemotherapy and radiation."

Reference from Alternative Cancer.us: "What happened to the Good Medicine?"

http://alternativecancer.us/doctors.htm

"In 1994 New York alternative healthcare advocates helped pass the Alternative Medical Practice Act designed to help guarantee that people would have access to alternative medical doctors by barring the State of New York from taking away the licenses of Alternative Medical Doctors just because they practiced alternative or non-conventional medicine. Despite the passing of this legislation, the Medical Board bureaucrats found a way to avoid the intent of the law. Alternative medical doctors were once again targeted and eliminated from medicine. Here are some examples....."

"Currently, (in California) it is a felony for a doctor to recommend any alternative cancer treatment..."

4. "Even today, the sugar industry still promotes the idea that sugar does not cause diabetes."

Reference from Mother Jones article "Big Sugar's Sweet Little Lies"
http://www.motherjones.com/environment/2012/10/sugar-industry-lies-campaign

"For 40 years, the sugar industry's priority has been to shed doubt on studies suggesting that its product makes people sick...."

"An international panel of experts—including Yudkin and Walter Mertz, head of the Human Nutrition Institute at the Department of Agriculture—testified that variations in sugar consumption were the best explanation for the differences in diabetes rates between populations, and that research by the USDA and others supported the notion that eating too much sugar promotes dramatic population-wide increases in the disease. One panelist, South African diabetes specialist George Campbell, suggested that anything more than 70 pounds per person per year—about half of what is sold in America today—would spark epidemics."

5. "In some schools, parents are even warned their children might be taken away by child protection agencies if they refuse to give their children drugs to treat ADHD."

In teaching about ADHD for the last 12 years I have personally heard examples of this from parents around the country.

Here is an example telling one parent's story whose son died from long-term use of Methylphenidate, Ritalin.

A. Reference from "Death From Ritalin: "The Truth Behind ADHD" http://www.ritalindeath.com

"Matthew's story started in a small town within Berkley, Michigan. While in first grade Matthew was evaluated by the school, who believed he had ADHD. The school social worker kept calling us in for meetings. One morning at one of these meetings while waiting for the others to arrive, Monica told us that if we refused to take Matthew to the doctor and get him on Ritalin, child protective services could charge us for neglecting his educational and emotional needs. My wife and I were intimidated and scared. We believed that there was a very real possibility of losing our children if we did not comply with the schools threats."

B. Reference from Natural News: "Medical mafia in Australia to force parents to medicate ADHD children"

http://www.naturalnews.com/034267_medical_mafia_Australia.html

"West Australian Labor MP, author, and anti-ADHD medication campaigner Martin Whitely is quoted in *News Tonight* as saying that ADHD drugs are "the only possible medical interventions" and that parents who refuse to use them "may see their child put in care."

'Earlier this year, a SWAT team raided the Detroit home of Maryanne

Godboldo for refusing to medicate her daughter with dangerous psychiatric drugs. These thugs actually kidnapped the young girl, who was eventually released after it was determined that Maryanne had every right to choose her own daughter's medical care."

C. "Reference from the National Alliance against Mandated Mental Health Screening and Psychiatric Drugging of Children: "Schools Can't Require ADHD Drugs" http://ritalindeath.com/New-Federal-Law.htm

"U.S. House overwhelmingly passed a bill 407-12 barring schools from requiring hyperactive children to use drug treatments as a condition for attending classes."

"This bill was designed to curb reports of school officials telling parents that disruptive kids must begin drug treatment for ADHD (attention-deficit hyperactivity disorder) in order to attend school."

"It is unknown how often schools have tried to make medication a condition of attending class."

"Rep. John Boehner (R-Ohio) says the House Education and Workforce Committee, which he leads, have received a number of complaints from parents."

Chapter Three: What is ADHD?

1. "ADHD is one of the most common neurodevelopmental disorder diagnosed in children and teens."
Reference from the Centers for Disease Control and Prevention (CDC): "Facts About ADHD"
http://www.cdc.gov/ncbddd/adhd/facts.html

2. "Data published by the Centers for Disease Control and Prevention reveals that in 2011, one out of five boys and one out of 11 girls were diagnosed with ADHD."
Reference from the Centers for Disease Control and Prevention (CDC)
http://www.cdc.gov/media/dpk/2013/dpk-ADHD-estimates-rise.html

"More than 1 in 10 (11%) US school-aged children had received an ADHD diagnosis by a health care provider by 2011, as reported by parents. 6.4 million children reported by parents to have ever received a health care provider diagnosis of ADHD, including:

1 in 5 high school boys
1 in 11 high school girls"

3. "Autism, which often goes hand and hand with ADHD occurs five times more in boys."

A. Reference from CDC: Autism Spectrum Disorder
http://www.cdc.gov/ncbddd/autism/data.html
"ASD is almost 5 times more common among boys (1 in 42) than among girls (1 in 189)."

B. Reference from Psych Central: "ADHD Kids Often Show Autistic Traits"

http://psychcentral.com/news/2013/10/18/adhd-kids-often-show-autistic-traits/60851.html

C. "Children with attention-deficit hyperactivity disorder (ADHD) often exhibit autistic traits, which can lead to even greater problems with socialization, according to new research presented at the 26th European College of Neuropsychopharmacology (ECNP) Congress.

Previous research has shown that children with autism spectrum disorder (ASD) often also have a diagnosis of ADHD. This new study suggests that the reverse may also be true."

4. "The CDC reports that one out of 42 boys is diagnosed with autism."

A. Reference from CDC: Autism Spectrum Disorder
http://www.cdc.gov/ncbddd/autism/data.html
"ASD is almost 5 times more common among boys (1 in 42) than among girls (1 in 189)."

B. Reference from Reuters: "CDC Now Estimates That One in Fifty Children Has Autism Diagnosis"

http://www.pediastaff.com/blog/cdc-now-estimates-that-one-in-fifty-children-has-autism-diagnosis-13339

5. "Just 30 years ago, one in 10,000 children had autism."

Reference from Autism Science Foundation: "How common is Autism?"

http://www.autismsciencefoundation.org/what-is-autism/how-common-is-autism

"In the 1980's autism prevalence was reported as 1 in 10,000. In the nineties, prevalence was 1 in 2500 and later 1 in 1000."

6. "If your ADHD develops into Parkinson's disease as it did for me, then the odds of experiencing some form of cognitive impairment are one out of two."

Reference from the Parkinson Foundation's booklet on "Mind. Mood, & Memory"

http://www3.parkinson.org/site/DocServer/Mind_Mood_Memory.pdf;jsessionid=021343814F21E824805C4F1CC8A3B778.app347a?docID=191

"While approximately 50% of patients with PD will experience some form of cognitive impairment, not all individuals will be diagnosed with full-blown dementia."

Chapter Four: What Causes ADHD?

1. "Some say bad parenting causes ADHD. Others say it is the genes."

A. Reference from Huffington Post: 'Ritalin Gone Wrong: Is ADHD Caused by Bad Parenting?"

http://www.huffingtonpost.com/2012/02/06/ritalin-gone-wrong_n_1257386.html

"Dr. L Alan Sroufe has been fanning the flames of parental guilt lately by suggesting that one major cause of ADHD in children is... their parents.

This latest round came in the form of a New York Times Op-Ed piece titled "Ritalin Gone Wrong" in which Sroufe, who is a psychology professor emeritus at the University of Minnesota, declared that too many kids are on drugs to treat the condition. Three million children would not be taking the medication, he wrote, if their parents hadn't "derailed" them psychologically in the first place."

B. Reference from Psychology Today: "Why French Kids Don't Have ADHD"

http://www.psychologytoday.com/blog/suffer-the-children/201203/why-french-kids-dont-have-adhd

"Is ADHD a biological-neurological disorder? Surprisingly, the answer to this question depends on whether you live in France or in the United States. In the United States, child psychiatrists consider ADHD to be a biological disorder with biological causes. The preferred treatment is also biological—psycho stimulant medications such as Ritalin and Adderall.

French child psychiatrists, on the other hand, view ADHD as a medical condition that has psycho-social and situational causes. Instead of treating children's focusing and behavioral problems with drugs, French doctors prefer to look for the underlying issue that is causing the child distress—not in the child's brain but in the child's social context. They then choose to treat the underlying social context problem with psychotherapy or family counseling. This is a very different way of seeing things from the American tendency to attribute all symptoms to a biological dysfunction such as a chemical imbalance in the child's brain."

C. Other References:

a. What Causes ADHD: Myths vs. Facts

http://www.healthcentral.com/adhd/cf/slideshows/adhd-myths-vs-facts

b. How Many People Believe ADHD is Caused by Poor Parenting: http://parenting.blogs.nytimes.com/2012/05/04/

how-many-people-believe-a-d-h-d-is-caused-by-poor-parent-ing/?_php=true&_type=blogs&_r=0

c. What Causes ADHD? http://www.netdoctor.co.uk/adhd/whatcausesadhd.htm

2. "There are also those who minimize the epidemic of ADHD saying it is over-diagnosed to justify selling more drugs to children."

Reference from The New York Times article "The Selling of Attention-deficit Disorder"

http://www.nytimes.com/2013/12/15/health/the-selling-of-attention-deficit-disorder.html

"The numbers make it look like an epidemic. Well, it's not. It's preposterous," Dr. Conners, a psychologist and professor emeritus at Duke University, said in a subsequent interview. "This is a concoction to justify the giving out of medication at unprecedented and unjustifiable levels."

3. "Others claim that ADHD is merely psychological and not a physical impairment of the brain."

Reference from http://www.medhelp.org/posts/Child-Behavior/ADHD-Physical-or-Psychological/show/275691

"My daughter's pediatrician said ADHD is generally a psychological problem and therefore would not even begin to address the issue with me but rather steered me in the direction of mental health care.

Is this true? Is it an emotional/psychological condition treated as a physical disorder so there won't be as much stigma attached to it?"

4. "Modern brain scans can now detect clear differences in the ADHD brain verses the non-ADHD brain."

Reference from The Washington Post, "Brain Scans Link ADHD to Biological Flaw Tied to Motivation" Katherine Ellison, September 22, 2009

http://www.washingtonpost.com/wp-dyn/content/article/2009/09/21/AR2009092103100.html

"The imaging showed that, in people with ADHD, the receptors and transporters are significantly less abundant in mid-brain structures composing the so-called reward pathway, which is involved in associating stimuli with pleasurable expectations."

5. "Acetaminophen inhibits the natural production of glutathione, which is produced by your liver to protect the brain from free radical oxidation."

Reference from PubMed: "Glutathione reductase is inhibited by acetaminophen-glutathione conjugate in vitro." June 19, 2009

"We found that glutathione reductase, the essential enzyme of the antioxidant system, was dose-dependently inhibited by the product of acetaminophen metabolism..."

6. "When used to suppress fevers, this commonly used medicine (acetaminophen) suppresses your brain's natural ability to heal itself.

A. Reference from Rudolf Steiner Health Center: "Overheating Therapy"

http://www.steinerhealth.org/health/fever-therapy/

" 'Give me a chance to create fever and I will cure any disease,' said the great physician, Parmenides, 2,000 years ago."

"Fever is one of the body's own defensive and healing forces, created and sustained for the deliberate purpose of restoring health. The high temperature speeds up metabolism, inhibits the growth of the invading virus or bacteria, and literally burns the enemy with heat."

B. Reference from Huffington Post: "Fever Increases Immune System Defense, Study Shows" 11/3/11

http://www.huffingtonpost.com/2011/11/03/fever-immune-system-cells_n_1074445.html

Researchers from Roswell Park Cancer Institute found that a higher body temperature can help our immune systems to work better and harder against infected cells. The finding was published in the *Journal of Leukocyte Biology*.

7. "Children and adults with ADHD, bipolar and autism, as well those who suffer from dementia, Parkinson's disease and Alzheimer's disease have low glutathione production."

A. Reference from the Journal of Restorative Medicine 2013 by William Shaw: "Evidence that Increased Acetaminophen use in Genetically Vulnerable Children Appears to be a Major Cause of the Epidemics of Autism, Attention-deficit with Hyperactivity, and Asthma"

http://www.greatplainslaboratory.com/home/eng/articles/Evidence-that-increased-Acetaminophen-use.pdf

"It appears that the marked increase in the rate of autism, asthma, and attention-deficit with hyperactivity throughout much of the world may be largely caused by the marked increase in the use of acetaminophen in genetically and/or metabolically susceptible children, and the use of acetaminophen by pregnant women."

"The marked increases in the incidences of autism, asthma, and attention-deficit disorder in the United States coincide with the replacement of aspirin by acetaminophen in the 1980s. The characteristic loss of Purkinje cells in the brains of people with autism is consistent with depletion of brain glutathione due to excess acetaminophen usage, which leads to premature brain Purkinje cell death."

B. Reference from US National Library of Medicine: A role for glutathione in the pathophysiology of bipolar disorder and schizophrenia?

http://www.ncbi.nlm.nih.gov/pubmed/19689277

The tripeptide, glutathione (gamma-glutamylcysteinylglycine) is the primary endogenous free radical scavenger in the human body. When glutathione (GSH) levels are reduced there is an increased potential for cellular oxidative stress, characterized by an increase and accruement of reactive oxygen species (ROS). Oxidative stress has been implicated in the pathology of schizophrenia and bipolar disorder. This could partly be caused by alterations in dopaminergic and glutamatergic activity that are implicated in these illnesses.

C. Reference from US National Library of Medicine: "N-acetyl cysteine restores brain glutathione loss."

http://www.ncbi.nlm.nih.gov/pmc/articles/PMC3482580/

"Oxidative stress and reduced brain levels of glutathione have been implicated in schizophrenia and bipolar disorder."

D. Reference from US National Library of Medicine: "Cellular glutathione peroxidase in human brain: cellular distribution, and its potential role in the degradation of Lewy bodies in Parkinson's disease and dementia with Lewy bodies"

http://www.ncbi.nlm.nih.gov/pubmed/18853169

"Glutathione peroxidase (GPx-1) is regarded as one of the mammalian cell's main antioxidant enzymes inactivating hydrogen peroxide and protecting against oxidative stress. Using control, Parkinson's disease (PD), and dementia with Lewy bodies tissue (DLB) we have shown that GPx-1 is a 21-kD protein under reducing conditions in all tissues examined but is not in high abundance in human brain."

E. Reference from US National Library of Medicine: "Metabolic biomarkers of increased oxidative stress and impaired methylation capacity in children with autism."

http://www.ncbi.nlm.nih.gov/pubmed/15585776

"This study looked at the metabolism of autistic children. Impairments in the methylation cycle, a very critical part of our body's functioning, were found. Because of this problem in the methylation cycle, autistic children are predisposed to low glutathione, which prevents them from detoxifying normally. It was also found that certain co-enzymes, all non-pharmaceutical, support that cycle."

F. Reference from US National Library of Medicine: "Dysregulation of glutathione homeostasis in neurodegenerative diseases."

http://www.ncbi.nlm.nih.gov/pubmed/23201762

"Dysregulation of glutathione homeostasis and alterations in glutathione-dependent enzyme activities are increasingly implicated in the induction and progression of neurodegenerative diseases, including Alzheimer's, Parkinson's and Huntington's diseases…"

G. Addition references to glutathione and healthy brain function:

1. Lang CA, Naryshkin S, Schneider DL, et al. Low blood glutathione in healthy aging adults. J Lab Clin Med 1992; 120: 720-25. [PubMed] 2. Julius M, Lang CA, Gleiberman L, et al. Glutathione and morbidity in a community-based ample of elderly. J Clin Epidemiol 1994; 47: 1021-26. [PubMed]

3. Fletcher RH, Fletcher SW. Glutathione and aging: ideas and evidence. Lancet 1994; 344: 1379-80. [PubMed]

4. Beutler E, Gelbart T. Plasma glutathione in health and in patients with malignant disease. J Lab Clin Med 1985; 105: 581-84. [PubMed] 5 Nourooz-Zadeh J, Tajaddinni-Sarmadi J, Wolff SP. Measurement of plasma hydroperoxide concentrations by the ferrous oxidation-xylenol orange assay in conjunction with triphenylphosphine. Anal Biochem 1994; 220: 403-09. [PubMed]

8. "Chronic exposure to known neurotoxins like MSG (monosodium glutamate) and HVP (Hydrolyzed Vegetable Protein) contributes to the oxidative stress that causes ADHD."
Reference from MSG Myth: "ADD, ADHD, And Autism"

http://www.msgmyth.com/add_adhd.html

"Neurochem Int. Aug-Sep, 200; 37 (23): 199-206). It states, "In the absence of glutamate, neurons are unaffected by acute exposure to mercury... Co-application of non-toxic concentrations of methylmercury and glutamate leads to typical appearance of neuronal lesions associated with excitotoxic stimulation (Matyja and Albrecht 1993.)"

9. "ADHD and dementia both share one common denominator: they can be triggered by heavy metal like mercury."

Reference from Psychology Today: "Are ADHD and Dementia Preventable Diseases?"

http://www.psychologytoday.com/blog/why-can-t-i-get-better/201312/are-adhd-and-dementia-preventable-diseases

10. "High blood sugar levels contribute to ADHD by causing free radical oxidation to brain neurons and chronic inflammation."

Reference from Neurosurgery: "The influence of hyperglycemia on neurological outcome in patients..." by Rovlias A, Kotsou S., 2000 Feb;46(2):335-42; discussion 342-3

http://www.ncbi.nlm.nih.gov/pubmed/10690722

"Traumatic brain injury is associated with a stress response that includes hyperglycemia"

11. "This downregulation of dopamine receptors (due to high sugar levels) has been linked to ADHD.

A. Reference from Science Daily "Low Levels of Dopamine Markers Underlie Symptoms"

http://www.sciencedaily.com/releases/2009/09/090908193432.htm

"The results clearly showed that, relative to the healthy control subjects, the ADHD patients had lower levels of dopamine receptors and transporters in the accumbens and mid-brain — two key regions of the brain directly involved in processing motivation and reward."

"The findings may also help explain why ADHD patients are more likely than control subjects to develop drug abuse disorders and conditions such as obesity."

"Said Wang: "Other studies from our group suggest that patients who abuse drugs or overeat may be unconsciously attempting to compensate for a deficient reward system by boosting their dopamine levels."

B. Reference from Daily Mail: "Sugar-laden junk food activates the same region of the brain affected by heroin and cocaine."

http://www.dailymail.co.uk/health/article-2402746/Food-addiction-DOES-ex

"A study Boston University found that high sugar snacks activated an area of brain called the nucleus accumbens that is also stimulated by class A drugs."

C. Reference from the University of Texas at Austin. http://www.utexas.edu/research/asrec/dopamine.html

"This overstimulation (class A drugs) leads to the down regulation of dopamine receptors."

12. "In addition, high insulin levels, which result from high blood sugar levels, inhibit glutathione production making the baby's brain more vulnerable to oxidative stress caused by toxic metals like lead, mercury and aluminum."

A. Reference from NBC News: "High blood sugar in pregnancy puts baby at risk"

http://www.nbcnews.com/id/19374297/ns/health-pregnancy/t/high-blood-sugar-pregnancy-puts-baby-risk/#.U73M4JG2-ao

"The newborns also were more likely to have low blood sugar levels and high insulin levels if their mothers' blood sugar levels were higher. The problems can lead to obesity, diabetes and high blood pressure later in life."

"High insulin levels are known to inhibit glutathione, which protects the brain from free radical oxidation as well as detoxify the body."

B. Reference from PubMed: "Intracellular reduced glutathione content in normal and type 2 diabetic erythrocytes: Effect of Insulin."

http://www.ncbi.nlm.nih.gov/pubmed/11596865

"The GSH (glutathione) content was significantly lower ($p < 0.001$) in type 2 diabetic patients as compared to normal individuals."

13. "Violence and criminal behavior is directly linked to lead poisoning in the brain"

Reference from Forbes: "How Lead Caused America's Violent Crime Epidemic."

http://www.forbes.com/sites/alexknapp/2013/01/03/how-lead-caused-americas-violent-crime-epidemic/

"Decades of research has shown that lead poisoning causes significant and probably irreversible damage to the brain. Not only does lead degrade cognitive abilities and lower intelligence, it also degrades a person's ability to make decisions by damaging areas of the brain responsible for "emotional regulation, impulse control, attention, verbal reasoning, and mental flexibility."

"Toddlers who ingested high levels of lead in the '40s and '50s really were more likely to become violent criminals in the '60s, '70s, and '80s."

"Starting in the 1960s, America saw a huge increase in levels of violent crime that peaked in the early 1990s, then steadily declined, and continues to decline today. All of it points to one simple idea: violent crime rose as a result of lead poisoning because of leaded gasoline. It declined because of lead abatement policies."

"...even moderately high levels of lead exposure are associated with aggressivity, impulsivity, ADHD, and lower IQ. And right there, you've practically defined the profile of a violent young offender."

14. "ADHD is linked to high mercury levels in the brain"

A. Reference from Medical News Today: "Prenatal Mercury intake Linked to ADHD"

http://www.medicalnewstoday.com/articles/251293.php

"A new study shows slight mercury exposure during pregnancy could be linked to a higher risk of ADHD-related behaviors."

"The current study examined 400 children born in New Bedford, Massachusetts between 1993 and 1998. After the mothers gave birth, their hair samples were collected and analyzed for mercury by the researchers. A survey was also given to measure their fish consumption during pregnancy. Researchers performed a follow-up eight years later with the children, conducting standardized tests to check if they exhibited behaviors related to ADHD."

"Findings showed an elevated risk of childhood ADHD-related behaviors with raised maternal hair mercury levels."

"These findings underscore the difficulties pregnant women face when trying to balance the nutritional benefits of fish intake with the potential detriments of low-level mercury exposure."

15. " Alzheimer's disease and dementia are linked to high aluminum levels in the brain"

A. Reference from PubMed: "Aluminum ingestion—is it related to dementia."

http://www.ncbi.nlm.nih.gov/pubmed/1842454

"Elevated levels of aluminum in brain tissue have been found in demented patients with Alzheimer's disease, with ALS-PD complex of Guam and with dialysis encephalopathy."

B. Reference from Rense.com: "Alzheimer's Again Linked to Aluminum"

http://www.rense.com/general37/alum.htm

"In patients having Alzheimer's disease the brain is somewhat shrunken and, on postmortem examination, a definite loss of nervous tissue is noted. Examination of the brain tissues under a microscope reveals small bundles of material called senile plaques, scattered throughout the tissues. The more plaques that are present, the worse is the mental condition of the patient. Chemical analysis reveals the presence of the metal aluminum at the core of each plaque and within many of the cells found in the plaques. Evidence is accumulating to indicate that aluminum may be involved in the formation of the plaques, and it is therefore a prime suspect as the initial cause of the disease."

"Five population studies now link Alzheimer's disease to aluminum in drinking water. As early as 1885, aluminum was shown to be toxic to the nervous tissues of animals. Aluminum can also produce a degeneration of the nervous tissues in cats and rabbits that resembles in some ways that seen in the brains of human patients with Alzheimer's disease. Patients with diseased kidneys accumulate large amounts of aluminum in their bodies from medications and from kidney-machine solutions that have been used until recently. This accumulation results in a severe mental deterioration."

C. Reference from The Telegraph: "Is Aluminum really a silent killer?" Feb, 6, 2014

http://www.telegraph.co.uk/health/9119528/Is-aluminium-really-a-silent-killer.html

"His research has led him to believe that accumulation of aluminum in the body is a risk factor not only for Alzheimer's disease but may also be linked to other neurological conditions such as Parkinson's and multiple sclerosis – and he believes that the Cross inquest will reignite debate about the potential risk of Alzheimer's in particular."

"Carole Cross died of a type of Alzheimer's known as congophilic amyloid angiopathy (CAA), an aggressive form of the disease that is extremely rare and practically unheard of for someone her age," he says. "Her case demonstrates aluminum's potential to aggravate and possibly accelerate ongoing disease. There is little doubt in my mind that the huge amounts of aluminum in her brain contributed significantly to the early onset of the condition."

"Aluminum, he argues, is now added to or used in almost everything we eat, drink, inject or absorb. At high levels, it is an established neurotoxin – yet no one knows whether the levels we are ingesting are safe."

"Bread and bakery products contain relatively high levels of aluminum salts. Other products with added aluminum include fizzy drinks, children's sweets, antiperspirants (where they inhibit the sweat glands), some processed cheeses, toothpaste, sunscreen, talcs and cosmetics, some over-the-counter medications and vaccines. It is also found as a contaminant in infant formulas. Soya formulas have been found to contain 10 times more aluminum than milk-based formulas."

16. "Numerous research studies link sugar consumption to the symptoms of ADHD."

Reference from Postgraduate Medicine: "Attention-deficit/ Hyperactivity Disorder: "Is it Time to Reappraise the Role of Sugar Consumption?" *Richard J. Johnson, MD; Mark S. Gold, MD; David R. Johnson, PhD; Takuji Ishimoto, MD; Miguel A. Lanaspa, PhD; Nancy R. Zahniser, PhD; and Nicole M. Avena, PhD* **DOI:** 10.3810/pgm.2011.09.2458

http://www.postgradmed.org/doi/10.3810/pgm.2011.09.2458

"We review preclinical and clinical data suggesting overlaps among ADHD, sugar and drug addiction, and obesity. Further, we present the hypothesis that the chronic effects of excessive sugar intake may lead to alterations in mesolimbic dopamine signaling, which could contribute to the symptoms associated with ADHD."

17. "A myriad of brain scans have proven that excessive dopamine stimulation due to street drugs like cocaine, crack, heroin and methamphetamines change and injure the brain."

Reference from Amen Clinic: "Brain Pollution and the Real Reason You Shouldn't Use Drugs"

http://www.amenclinics.com/about-us-23/the-science-2/spect-gallery/item/alcohol-and-drug-abuse

"The most common similarity among drug and alcohol abusers is that the brain has an overall toxic look to it. In general, the SPECT Scan studies look less active, more shriveled, and overall less healthy. A "scalloping effect" is common amongst drug abusing brains. Normal brain patterns show smooth activity across the cortical surface."

18. "Similar changes take place in the brain when taking prescribed stimulant drugs for ADD and ADHD."

A. Reference from Learn Genetics: Ritalin and Cocaine
http://learn.genetics.utah.edu/content/addiction/ritalin/

"But because Ritalin is a stimulant like cocaine, it may cause undesirable changes in the brain over time. It also has the potential for abuse, and because it's a legal prescription drug, many wrongly assume that it is not dangerous."

B. Reference from Wikipedia: "Long-term Effects of ADHD drugs" http://en.wikipedia.org/wiki/Methylphenidate

"A small study of just under 100 children that assessed long-term outcome of stimulant use found that 6% of children became psychotic after months or years of stimulant therapy."

C. Reference from Live Science: "Ritalin, ADHD Drugs, May Spur Brain Changes: Study Suggests" by Rachael Rettner, May 15, 2013

http://www.livescience.com/32044-adhd-drug-treatment-brain-changes.html

"The study involved 18 adults with ADHD who had their brains scanned twice: once at the beginning of the study before any drug treatment, and once at the end of the study after one year of taking Ritalin."

"Among these participants, there was a 24 percent increase in the number of dopamine transporters in some areas of the brain.

"Dopamine transporters, on the other hand, clear dopamine after the chemical has sent a signal. Thus, more dopamine transporters could mean that dopamine gets cleared more quickly, particularly during times when patients stop taking their medications."

"This could result in more severe inattention and the need for higher doses of medication,"

" In contrast, a group of healthy participants who did not take Ritalin had no increase in dopamine transporters after one year."

D. Reference from PubMed: "Dopamine transport function is elevated in cocaine users." J Neurochem. 2002 Apr;81(2):292-300

http://www.ncbi.nlm.nih.gov/pubmed/12064476

"....we present evidence that DAT function is elevated by chronic cocaine abuse."

19. "Fifty to sixty percent of college kids take Ritalin or Adderall."

Reference from CBS News "60 Minutes: 'Popping Pills A Popular Way To Boost Brain Power"

http://www.cbsnews.com/news/
popping-pills-a-popular-way-to-boost-brain-power/

"Among Upper Classes, 50-60 percent Using ADD/ADHD Drugs Ritalin, Adderall"

20. "Thirty to fifty percent of adolescents in drug rehab centers have used Ritalin."

Reference from the Christian Science Monitor by Alexandra Marks: "Ritalin becoming school yard hustlers' newest product" Oct 30, 2000

".... a DEA study of Wisconsin, South Carolina, and Indiana found that about 30 to 50 percent of teens in drug treatment centers said they had used methylphenidate to get high, although not as their primary drug of abuse."

"Ritalin is interchangeable with amphetamine and methamphetamine, and all of them produce much the same effect as cocaine."

21. "This change makes the search for extra stimulation override other priorities."

Reference from Huff Post Science, February 7, "Cocaine Rewires Brain, Overrides Decision-Making After Just One Use, Says Study"

2014http://ajp.psychiatryonline.org/article.aspx?articleID=166820

"While similar studies have revealed such rewiring in long-term use, the new study's results are especially alarming, showing that the brain can be altered after one dose."

22. "A report published in 2005 by neurologist George A. Ricaurte and his team at the Johns Hopkins University School of Medicine is even more damning to ADHD meds."

Reference from Scientific American: "Do ADHD Drugs Take a Toll on the Brain?" by Edmund S. Higgins, July/August 2009

https://secure.suu.edu/faculty/barney/PSY%204320/
Interesting%20Articles/ADHD%20Drugs%20Affect%20the%20
Brain.pdf

"With the expanded and extended use of stimulants comes mounting concern that the drugs might take a toll on the brain over the long run. Indeed, a smattering of recent studies, most of them involving animals, hint that stimulants could alter the structure and function of the brain in ways that may depress mood, boost anxiety and, contrary to their short-term effects, lead to cognitive deficits. Human studies already indicate the medications can adversely affect areas of the brain that govern growth in children, and some researchers worry that additional harms have yet to be unearthed."

"Having ADHD is itself a risk factor for other mental health problems, but the possibility also exists that stimulant treatment during childhood might contribute to these high rates of accompanying diagnoses."

23. "According to Professor William Carlezon of Harvard University ADHD medication oxidizes the nucleus accumbens in the developing brain leading to a loss of drive in adulthood."

Reference from article by Leonard Sax author of Boys Adrift. I highly recommend this book to understand why boys today are falling behind.

http://untotheone.com/articles/epitomes/boys-adrift/

24. "This research was confirmed by research at Brown University, University of Michigan, University of Pittsburgh, South Carolina, and universities in Holland, Sweden, and Italy and the Netherlands."

References from:

A. University of Michigan: T.H.E. Robinsons and B. Lolb: Structural plasticity associated with exposure to drugs of abuse." Neuropharmacology. 2004;47 Suppl 1:33-46.

http://www.ncbi.nlm.nih.gov/pubmed/15464124

B. Medical University of South Caroline: P.W. Kalivas, N.Volkow, J Seamans, "Unmanageable motivation in addiction: a pathology in prefrontal," Neuron. 2005 Mar 3;45(5):647-50.

http://www.ncbi.nlm.nih.gov/pubmed/15748840 Neuron. 2005 Mar 3;45(5):647-50.

C. University of Pittsburgh: S.P. Onn and A. A. Grace:, "Amphetamine withdrawal alters bistable states and cellular coupling in rat prefrontal cortex and nucleus accumbens neurons recorded in vivo." J Neurosci. 2000 Mar 15;20(6):2332-45.

http://www.ncbi.nlm.nih.gov/pubmed/10704508

D. Brown University: Y. Li and J.A. Kaauer, "Repeated exposure to amphetamine disrupts dopaminergic modulation of excitatory synaptic plasticity and neurotransmission in nucleus accumbens," Synapse. 2004 Jan;51(1):1-10.http://www.ncbi.nlm.nih.gov/pubmed/14579420

E. Sweden: R. Diaz Heijtz, B. Kolb, and H. Forssberg, "Can a therapeutic dose of amphetamine during pre-adolescence modify the pattern of synaptic organization in the brain?," European Journal of Neuroscience, 16, Dec 2003, Vol 18, Issue 12, pages 3394-3399

http://onlinelibrary.wiley.com/doi/10.1046/j.0953-816X.2003.03067.x/abstract

F. Italy: G. Di Chiara, V. Bassareo, S. Fenu, M. A. De Luca and associates, "Dopamine and drug addiction: the nucleus accumbens shell connection," Neuropharmacology. 2004;47 Suppl 1:227-41.

http://www.ncbi.nlm.nih.gov/pubmed/15464140

G. Netherland: Louk J. M. J. Vanderschuren, E. Donne´ Schmidt, Taco J. De Vries, Caroline A. P. Van Moorsel, Fred J.H. Tilders, and Anton N. M. Schoffelmeer, "A Single Exposure to Amphetamine Is Sufficient to Induce Long- Term Behavioral,

Neuroendocrine, and Neurochemical Sensitization in Rats," The
Journal of Neuroscience, November 1, 1999, *19*(21):9579–9586
http://www.jneurosci.org/content/19/21/9579.full.pdf

**25. "A growing body of research reveals that "gaming" improves
creativity, decision-making and perception, improved hand-eye
coordination and improved vision for discerning gray tones."**
Reference from Wall Street Journal: "When Gamin Is Good
for You" Robert Lee Hotz, March 13, 2012
http://online.wsj.com/news/articles/SB100014240529702034
58604577263273943183932

**26. "The four-year process of learning to navigate the
streets of London actually increases the size of the brain called
the hippocampus, which has to do with memory"**
Reference from University College London: BBC News; "Taxi
drivers' brains grow on the job"
http://news.bbc.co.uk/2/hi/677048.stm
"The scientists also found part of the hippocampus grew
larger as the taxi drivers spent more time in the job."

**27. "Researchers at Indiana University using brain scans
reported that playing violent video games alters brain function in healthy young men after just a week of play, depressing
activity among regions associated with emotional control."**
Reference from Medscape Medical News: "Playing Violent
Video Games Changes Brain Function" Fran Lowry November
29,2011http://www.medscape.com/viewarticle/754368
"The researchers found that after 1 week of violent video
game play, the study group showed less activation in the left
inferior frontal lobe during the emotional task and less activation in the anterior cingulate cortex during the counting task,

compared with their baseline results and results in the control group."

"Their executive functioning abilities were decreased, and so were their cognitive functioning abilities,"

"The disturbances in brain activity that were manifested after a period of violent video gaming on fMRI are sobering, he added. "It's not just psychological, there is some underlying change that can actually be measured with imaging. These changes should not be dismissed."

28. "Other studies have found an association between compulsive gaming and being overweight, introverted and prone to depression."

Reference from Choose Help: "Adult Video Gamers Are Heavier, More Introverted and More Likely Depressed" John Lee, August 19, 2009

http://www.choosehelp.com/news/non-substance-addictions/adult-video-gamers-are-heavier-more-introverted-and-more-likely-depressed.html

"Researchers at the CDC conducted a snapshot study of American adult video gamers, and found that on average, video game players have higher BMI scores, women gamers are more likely depressed and all gamers (on average) rely on the internet for social support at the expense of real world sociability."

"Dr. James Weaver III of the CDC, a lead researcher in the study, reported that the results taken from an adult population, "appear consistent with earlier research on adolescents that linked video game playing to a sedentary lifestyle and overweight status and mental health concerns." He says that their study did not attempt to find the good and bad in video game playing, only to, "see better how adults play video games."

29. "In the case of video games, this stimulation increases blood blow to the "nucleus accumbens" or pleasure center in the middle of the brain. At the same times blood flow decreases to the prefrontal cortex."

Reference from Science Direct: "Sustained Decrease in Oxygenated Hemoglobin During Video Games in the Dorsal Prefrontal Cortex: A NIRS study of children," Goh Matsuda and Kazuo Hiraki, *Neuroimage,* volume 29, pp. 706–711, 2006.

"These findings suggest that game-related oxyHb decrease in DPFC is a common phenomenon to adults and children at least older than 7 years old, and we suggest that this probably results from attention demand from the video games rather than from subject's age and performance."

30. "Extended time on a video game increases our ability to play the game but decreases our control over automatic impulses."

Reference from Comprehensive psychiatry: "Brain activity and desire for internet video game play."

http://www.ncbi.nlm.nih.gov/pmc/articles/PMC3039876/

"The current study provides information with respect brain changes that support the motivation to continue playing an internet video game in the early stages. Based on previous studies of cue-induced craving in substance abusers, the present findings also suggest the neural circuitry that mediates cue-induced desire for internet video games is similar to that observed following cue presentation to individuals with substance dependence."

31. "A recent brain imaging study by researchers at Stanford's school of medicine suggests that men are more vulnerable to addiction to video games."

Reference from Video Game Addiction: "Boys and Video Games: A Natural Attraction?"

http://www.video-game-addiction.org/boys-and-video-games.html

"The researchers also found greater activation in male brains in three brain structures - the nucleus accumbens, amygdala, and orbitofrontal cortex - and that the brain activity increased according to how much territory they had gained. The female brains showed no such correlation."

32. "The neural circuitry that mediates desire for internet video games is similar to that observed with substance dependence."

Reference from Comprehensive psychiatry: "Brain activity and desire for internet video game play."

http://www.ncbi.nlm.nih.gov/pmc/articles/PMC3039876/

"Based on previous studies of cue-induced craving in substance abusers, the present findings also suggest the neural circuitry that mediates cue-induced desire for internet video games is similar to that observed following cue presentation to individuals with substance dependence."

33. "In a study of 300 children whose mothers received Pitocin at birth to induce labor, 67.1% of the children were diagnosed with ADHD."

Reference from Natural News: "Pitocin induced labor doubles the risk of ADHD."

http://www.naturalnews.com/033259_pitocin_ADHD.html

"The occurrence of ADHD in the pitocin group was 67.1% as opposed to 35.6% in the non-exposure group."

34. "A study in North Carolina reported that women whose labor was induced were 16% more likely to have a child later diagnosed with autism"

Reference from USA Today: "Brain changes of autism may begin in the womb"

http://www.usatoday.com/story/news/nation/2013/08/12/
autism-labor-induction/2641391/

"Women whose labor was sped up were 16% more likely to have a child later diagnosed with autism, the study found. Those whose labor was both induced and augmented were 27% more likely to have an autistic child."

35. "Twenty-five percent of mothers in the US receive Pitocin during labor."

Reference from Transforming Maternity Care: "What Are Some Factors Driving Use Of Induced Labor In The United States?"

http://transform.childbirthconnection.org/reports/
listeningtomothers/induction/

"Many women report experiencing pressure from a care provider to have an induction. Overall, 15% of mothers reported experiencing pressure from a care provider to have labor induced. This rose to 25% among mothers who experienced a medical induction compared with 8% among those who did not have an induction."

36. "In some hospitals up to ninety percent of mothers receive Pitocin."

Reference from Bellybelly.com: "The Risks Of Labour Induction"

http://www.bellybelly.com.au/birth/induction-of-labour-to-induce-or-not-induce#.Uvj8upFf-ao

"...some hospitals, mainly private ones, have a 90% induction rate termed 9 a.m. to 5 p.m. obstetrics, so the care-giver is not woken overnight to attend births."

37. In my book *Why Mars and Venus Collide* I explore in great detail how balanced brain chemicals can lower stress and increase oxytocin levels.

38. "Research reveals that healthy production of neurotransmitters is directly associated with the release of oxytocin."

Reference from F. Moos , P. Richard .: "Excitatory effect of dopamine on oxytocin," Brain Res. 1982 Jun 10;241(2):249-60

http://www.ncbi.nlm.nih.gov/pubmed/7104713

"So, we can postulate that dopamine regulates the reflex release of oxytocin and vasopressin in the hypothalamus."

39. "Statistics reveal a greater risk of ADHD in children of divorced parents, particularly when boys are missing the regular influence of a father or mothers are unable to find happiness."

Reference from University of North Carolina at Charlotte: Family Structure, Household Income, and Mental/Behavioral Wellness in Children with ADHD

Using Data from the 2002 National Health Survey

http://www.psych.uncc.edu/cdfernal/ADHA%20Child%20&%20Family%20K%20Kitts.htm

"More children diagnosed with ADHD are from single mother families, whereas more children without an ADHD diagnosis are from dual parent families."

40. "The presence of a father figure increases the brain chemical dopamine while the presence of a happy mother can also generate this brain chemical."

A. Reference from Neuroscience: "Father Absence in the Monogamous California Mouse Impairs Social Behavior and Modifies Dopamine and Glutamate Synapses in the Medial Prefrontal Cortex" by Francis R. Bambico, Baptiste Lacoste, Patrick R. Hattan and Gabriella Gobbi

http://cercor.oxfordjournals.org/content/early/2013/11/24/cercor.bht310.abstract

"We thus demonstrate that, during critical neurodevelopmental periods, paternal deprivation leads to sex-dependent abnormalities in social and reward-related behaviors that are associated with disturbances in cortical dopamine and glutamate neurotransmission."

B. Reference from Journal of Neuroendocrinology: Maternal Neglect: Oxytocin, Dopamine and the Neurobiology of Attachment, by Lane Strathearn, MBBS FRACP PhD

http://www.ncbi.nlm.nih.gov/pmc/articles/PMC3319675/#!po=13.6364

"Maternal neglect, including physical and emotional neglect, is a pervasive public health challenge with serious long-term effects on child health and development."

" ...A human PET study likewise showed that low self-reported maternal care was associated with an elevated dopamine response to stress."

"...prolonged maternal separation and isolation rearing of rat pups results in reduced dopamine transporter binding in the VS, elevated baseline dopamine levels and increased dopamine release in response to acute stress in adulthood. These animals also show enhanced sensitivity to psychostimulants such as cocaine, which activate dopaminergic neurons, and this may lead to increased vulnerability to addiction."

41. "A 2006 Dutch study found that erotica had the highest addictive potential of all internet applications."

Reference from Cyber Psychology Behavior: "Predicting compulsive Internet use: it's all about sex!" Meerkerk GJ, Van Den Eijnden RJ, Garretsen HF., 2006 Feb;9(1):95-103.

http://www.ncbi.nlm.nih.gov/pubmed/16497122

"The addictive potential of the different applications varies; erotica appears to have the highest potential."

42. "A study using brain scans at Cambridge University found that pornography addiction leads to the same brain activity as alcoholism or drug abuse."

Reference from Cambridge University:" Brain Scans Find Porn Addiction" by Valerie Voon, Channel 4 documentary, "Porn On The Brain"

http://yourbrainonporn.com/cambridge-university-brain-scans-find-porn-addiction

"We found greater activity in an area of the brain called the ventral striatum, which is a reward center, involved in processing reward, motivation and pleasure."

"When an alcoholic sees an ad for a drink, their brain will light up in a certain way and they will be stimulated in a certain way. We are seeing this same kind of activity in users of pornography."

43. "During normal intimate sexual intercourse the body releases four times more prolactin than from masturbation."

Reference from Biological Phycology: "The post-orgasmic prolactin increase following intercourse is greater than following masturbation and suggests greater satiety." Brody S, Krüger TH.2006 Mar;71(3):312-5. Epub 2005 Aug 10.

http://www.ncbi.nlm.nih.gov/pubmed/16095799%20

.."the magnitude of prolactin increase following intercourse is 400% greater than that following masturbation."

44. "As a result, internet porn can lead to a blunting of interest in sex with a real partner and an increased desire for more porn."

Reference from Your Brain On Porn: "What happens when you ejaculate too much."

http://www.yourbrainonporn.com/node/941

"These days, however, a bevy of novel mates begs for fertilization at a click. And when our brain grows less responsive, something even more stimulating is at the next tab. Are some guys losing touch with their "true libido?"

45. "Although it is still not accepted by mainstream medicine, holistic health practitioners recognize that children with ADHD and autism almost always have different degrees of indigestion caused by an excess of candida."

Reference from Food Renegade: "New Research Confirms ADHD Caused by Food" Kristen Michaelis

http://www.foodrenegade.com/
new-research-confirms-adhd-caused-by-food/

"Dr. McBride (Author of Gut and Psychology Syndrome) contends that the link between our digestion and neurological and psychological disorders is absolute. The theory is straight-forward. When the balance of "good" bacteria and yeast to "bad" bacteria and yeast in our digestive tract goes out of whack, a condition called "gut dysbiosis" occurs. The "bad" microorganisms produce toxins which weaken your immune system, tax your organs, and throw multiple body systems out of balance. The toxins can also increase the permeability of the gut lining, leading to IBS and a host of other digestive disorders."

46. "Taking probiotics after the use of antibiotics is one way to help avoid this outcome."

Reference from Advanced Mind Body Medicine, "Could yeast infections impair recovery from mental illness? A case study using micronutrients and olive leaf extract for the treatment of ADHD and depression." Rucklidge JJ., 2013 Summer;27(3):14-8.

47. "Children who were not breastfed or have taken lots of antibiotics have a higher risk of bowel disease and candida infestations."

Reference from About.com: "Can Breastfeeding An Infant Help Protect From Developing IBD?" Amber Tresca, November, 2013

http://ibdcrohns.about.com/od/dietandnutrition/f/breast-feedibd.htm

"Several studies show that people with IBD – Crohn's disease and ulcerative colitis – were more likely to not have been breast-fed as infants. The authors of one analysis of several studies on breastfeeding and IBD conclude that this protective effect may actually be underestimated."

48. "Studies have already confirmed that glyphosate alters and destroys beneficial intestinal bacteria in animals."

Reference from Gaia Health: "Glyphosate: Chronic Disease Degeneration." By Heidi Stevenson, April 26,2013

http://gaia-health.com/gaia-blog/2013-04-26/xxx-3/

"Glyphosate is assumed to be safe for humans. As a result, it's become the world's Best-selling herbicide. However, a groundbreaking study documents that it may actually be fueling the plague of chronic & immune diseases, including cancer and autism. This study documents the underlying systemic damage produced by glyphosate, then discusses how that damage leads to specific diseases."

"Gyphosate causes disruption of the shikimate pathway in gut bacteria, which results in a domino effect of pathology. It causes formation of excess shikimate, along with deficiencies of aromatic amino acids in plants."

49. "GMO glyphosate is also directly linked to ADHD and dopamine function because studies reveal that it inhibits the utilization of the amino acids phenylalanine, tryptophan and tyrosine."

Reference from Gaia Health: "Glyphosate: Chronic Disease Degeneration." By Heidi Stevenson, April 26,2013

http://gaia-health.com/gaia-blog/2013-04-26/xxx-3/

"Aromatic amino acids include phenylalanine, tryptophan, and tyrosine, among others. All three can be in short supply as a result of glyphosate's enzymatic suppression. Phenylalanine cannot be synthesized in the body and is required for synthesis of tyrosine. Its suppression results in a cascade of adverse effects, including of course, reduction in tyrosine."

50. "Glyphosate impairs the transport of sulfate for the liver to make glutathione."
Reference from Gaia Health: "Glyphosate: Chronic Disease Degeneration." By Heidi Stevenson, April 26,2013

http://gaia-health.com/gaia-blog/2013-04-26/xxx-3/

"Sulphate transport, the method by which sulphate is moved into and out of cells, is a delicate balance. When glyphosate is present, this balance becomes a tightrope walk. The problem is that both sulphate and glyphosate are kosmotropes, which can have a devastating impact on the blood."

51. "In addition glyphosates inhibit both the functioning of glutathione as well as the production of key hormones and vitamin D."
Reference from Natural Health: "Biotech industry produced GMOs block detoxification pathways

http://www.naturalhealth365.com/tag/biotech-industry

"Foods stuffs that are produced in fields that are sprayed by glyphosate carry residue of the chemical into the marketplace where they are consumed. In North America, bioengineered foods are ubiquitous and it is quite challenging for the average consumer to avoid them.

"It is well-established in the literature that glyphosate inhibit the CYP enzyme complex in human liver cells. Low levels of CYP enzymes complexes would result in a depletion of available glutathione and lowered capability of the organism to detox-ify from various environmental poisons such as nitrates and benzene."

"CYP enzymes are present in most tissues and play a criti-cal role in estrogen and testosterone production and metabolism, cholesterol synthesis and vitamin D metabolism. The inhibition of CYP enzymes increases the likelihood of adverse drug reactions (particularly to acetaminophen) and biotoxic accumulation."

52. "In 2003 scientists discovered that the popular pes-ticide "Endosulfan" blocks the action of testosterone in boys which in turn disrupts and delays the process of puberty."

Reference from Science News: "Slowing Puberty? Pesticide may hinder development in boys" Kate Ramsayer , volume 164, p. 372, 2003

This text can be read for free online at http://www.thefreelibrary. com/Pesticide+may+hinder+development+in+boys.-a0111856321

"Chronic exposure to a widely used pesticide may delay sexual maturity in boys, according to a new study in India. Endosulfan is an organochlorine (herbicide) used around the world to protect squash, melons, strawberries, and other produce. A 2001 report by the U.S. Environmental Protection Agency estimated that 1.4 million pounds of the pesticide are used annually on U.S. crops."

"Reproductive development of each boy was evaluated using a sexual maturity rating based on the size of the penis and testes and the development of pubic hair. After taking age into account, the researchers found that boys in Padre scored significantly lower on all three measurements than boys from the other village did."

53. "Atrazine, the most common pesticide used in American is now banned in Europe. Studies from University of California, Berkley have shown that Atrazine in minute amounts in water is making male frogs grow female ovaries."

Reference from Nature, Weekly Journal of Science: Feminization of male frogs in the wild"

http://www.nature.com/news/2002/021031/full/news021028-7.html

"Atrazine gives frogs male and female gonads, says field study."

54. "One of the major hormone disruptors for both boys and girls is the use of plastics. The increased levels of phthalate in the serum of young girls is directly linked to premature puberty in girls."

A. Reference from Environmental Health Perspectives: "Identification of phthalate esters in the serum of young Puerto Rican girls with premature breast development," Ivelisse Colón, Doris Caro, Carlos J. Bourdony, and Osvaldo Rosario, volume 108, pp. 895–900, 2000.

B. Reference from *Environmental Health Perspectives*: "Developmental abnormalities of the gonad and abnormal sex hormone concentrations in juvenile alligators from contaminated and control lakes in Florida," Louis J. Guillette Jr., Timothy S. Gross, Greg R. Masson, John M. Matter, H. Franklin Percival, and Allan R. Woodward, volume 102, pp. 680–688, 1994.

55. "In 2004, neuroscientists identified a crucial link between hormone disruptors and ADHD."

A. Reference from *Regulatory Peptides*: "Motor Hyperactivity Caused by a Deficit in Dopaminergic Neurons and the effects of Endocrine Disruptors: A study inspired by the physiological roles of PACAP in the brain," Yoshinori Masuo, Masatoshi Morita, Syuichi Oka, and Masami Ishido, volume 123, pp. 225–234, 2004.

http://www.ncbi.nlm.nih.gov/pubmed/15518916

"The changes in gene expression caused by treatment with endocrine disruptors ... suggest that the mechanisms underlying the induction of motor hyperactivity and/or compensatory changes in young adult rats..."

B. Reference from *Journal of Neurochemistry:* "Dicyclohexyl Phthalate causes Hyperactivity in the Rat Concomitantly with Impairment of Tyrosine Hydroxylase Immunoreactivity," Savato-Suzuki, S. Oka, E. Niki, and Masatoshi Morita, volume 91, pp. 69–76, 2004.

"Endocrine disruptors possibly exert effects on neuronal functions leading, in particular, to behavioral alterations."

56. "The EPA reports, "studies in laboratory animals suggest that fetuses exposed to phthalates, chemicals used in plastics, can have multiple health issues as adults, including infertility, issues with genitalia development and sperm production problems. Also there are epidemiological studies showing developmental changes in children including early puberty in boys and girls compared to previous generations."

Reference from United States Environmental Protection Agency: "Human Health: Early Life Exposures & Lifetime Health"

http://www.epa.gov/research/endocrinedisruption/early-life-exp.htm

"Chemicals that are being researched for such effects include organotins (used in PVC and as biocides), BPA (Bisphenol-A, present in canned food and many plastics) and PFOA (perfluorooctanoic acid, present in consumer products such as stain resistant carpet and waterproof jackets)."

57. "Scientists at Georgetown University and the University of Texas claim these new BPA- free plastics release chemicals having more estrogenic activity than the old BPA-containing products."

Reference from KQED Science: "Are BPA-Free Plastics Any Safer?" Mina Kim and Molly Samuel, March 5, 2014

"But lab tests by the Oakland-based advocacy group Center for Environmental Health, have found that the chemicals used to replace BPA may be just as harmful."

"Scientists with CertiChem, Georgetown University and the University of Texas, had already published a National Institutes of Health-funded study in 2011, testing estrogen exposure from a wide range of plastics, including baby bottles and other products advertised as BPA free. "In some cases," the researchers reported, "BPA-free products released chemicals having more EA [estrogenic activity] than did BPA-containing products."

58. "One third of Americans are so compromised in the gut that they cannot tolerate gluten"

Reference from NPR.ORG: Gluten Goodbye: One-Third of Americans Say There're Trying To Shun It" by Nancy Shute March 09, 2013

http://www.npr.org/blogs/thesalt/2013/03/09/173840841/gluten-goodbye-one-third-of-americans-say-theyre-trying-to-shun-it

"Right now 29 percent of the adult population says, 'I'd like to cut back or avoid gluten completely."

59. "By giving up gluten products many people have reduced or eliminated ADHD symptoms."

Reference from Mercola.com: "Child Have ADHD? Stop Feeding Them This" Dr. Mercola, November 02, 2011

http://articles.mercola.com/sites/articles/archive/2011/11/02/gluten-contribute-to-adhd.aspx

"There's evidence suggesting that gluten sensitivity may be at the root of many neurological and psychiatric conditions, including attention-deficit hyperactivity disorder (ADHD)."

"Eating gluten-containing grain may wreak havoc on your gut and manifest in symptoms related to your brain, including ADHD symptoms"

"A gluten-free diet may significantly improve ADHD symptoms"

60. "A multitude of studies have shown that for many adults and children food sensitivities are a major cause of ADHD."

A. Reference from ABC News: "ADHD From Allergy? Study Shows Benefit From Diet Changes" by Courtney Hutchison via Good Morning America

http://abcnews.go.com/Health/Allergies/adhd-food-allergy-case-restricting-diet/story?id=12832958

"In kids with ADHD, researchers found that putting them on a restrictive diet to eliminate possible, previously unknown food allergies or sensitivities decreased hyperactivity for 64 percent of kids."

B. Reference from US News: Allergies, Asthma Show Links to ADHD: Study" by Serena Gordon, Aug 23, 2013

http://health.usnews.com/health-news/news/articles/2013/08/23/allergies-asthma-show-links-to-adhd-study

"Of those in the study, boys newly diagnosed with ADHD were 40 percent more likely to have asthma, 50 percent more likely to have needed a prescription for allergy medicine and 50 percent more likely to have had a bacterial skin infection than other boys."

"They also found weaker associations between ADHD and cow's milk intolerance, and prescriptions for oral or topical corticosteroids, antibacterial or antifungal drugs."

C. Reference from Diagnosis - Diet: Food Sensitivities and ADHD By Georgia Ede MD

http://diagnosisdiet.com/food-sensitivities-and-adhd/

This is a great site as Dr. Ede lists a variety of simplified diets that have helped and sometimes cured ADHD.

61. "At the end of five weeks, 64 percent of the children on the restricted diet had significant improvement in their ADHD symptoms, while none of the control group had improvements."

Reference from ABC News: "ADHD From Allergy? Study Shows Benefit From Diet Changes" by Courtney Hutchison via Good Morning America

http://abcnews.go.com/Health/Allergies/adhd-food-allergy-case-restricting-diet/story?id=12832958

"In kids with ADHD, researchers found that putting them on a restrictive diet to eliminate possible, previously unknown food allergies or sensitivities decreased hyperactivity for 64 percent of kids."

62. "The impact of this environmental stress on our body along with any of the factors above contributes to the brain injury that gives rise to ADHD"

Reference from the US EPA: "Parallels between ADHD and Disorder and Behavioral Deficits Produced by Neurotoxic Exposure in Monkeys" Deborah C. Rice of the EPA.

http://www.ncbi.nlm.nih.gov/pmc/articles/PMC1637819/pdf/envhper00312-0043.pdf

"There are some parallels between the features of ADHD and the behavior of monkeys exposed developmentally to lead or polychlorinated biphenyls (PCBs), as evidenced by research from our laboratory."

63. "Children are more vulnerable to these neurotoxins because their brains are still developing."

Reference from Environmental Health: "One Chance to Develop a Brain: Neurotoxic chemicals and children's health" Fall 2008

http://www.environmentalhealth.ca/fall08brain.html

"A 'silent pandemic' is affecting the brain development of children."

64. "The bottom line is you only get one chance to develop a brain," said Philippe Grandjean, M.D., lead author of the study in an interview with WebMD. We have to protect children against chemical pollution because damage to a developing brain is irreversible."

Reference from Environmental Health: "One Chance to Develop a Brain: Neurotoxic chemicals and children's health" Fall 2008

http://www.environmentalhealth.ca/fall08brain.html

"In the nine month period when the fetal brain develops, growth occurs within "a tightly controlled time frame, in which each developmental stage has to be reached on schedule and in the correct sequence." This creates "windows of unique susceptibility to toxic interference" that can have permanent consequences, say Grandjean and co-author Philip J. Landrigan, a professor at Mount Sinai School of Medicine."

65. "Their research suggests that moms are passing on these toxic chemicals to their babies. These toxins match what scientists are finding in the umbilical cord of their babies once they are born."

Reference from CNN Health: "Toxic chemicals finding their way into the womb" Stephanie Smith, July 28, 2010

"Despite her best efforts to avoid anything unhealthy while she was pregnant with her son, Molly's blood tested high for mercury, a heavy metal that can cause brain damage to a developing fetus."

"Small studies by other groups are also finding common household chemicals in babies."

"The amount of chemicals measured in the cord blood of the babies seems to matter. The higher the concentration, the more the IQ among children seems to dip. The study is also being conducted among pregnant women in Poland and China, and finding similar results."

66. "Women who take Tylenol, which suppresses glutathione, have a much higher risk of giving birth to children with ADHD, behavior problems, poor language and motor skills and communication difficulties."

A. Reference from Natural News: When Pregnant Women take Tylenol, their children are more likely to be born with autism."

http://www.naturalnews.com/043087_Tylenol_autism_pregnant_women.html

"Expectant mothers who took the drug while pregnant to deal with headaches or mild fevers were found to be significantly more likely to bear children with behavioral problems, poor language and motor skills, and communication difficulties, compared to mothers who did not take the drug."

"The study included data on 48,000 Norwegian children whose mothers participated in a survey evaluating their medication use at weeks 17 and 30 of pregnancy, as well as at six months after giving birth. The survey also included a follow-up that looked at the children's developmental progress at three years of age, which was then compared to the mothers' drug intake during the later stages of their pregnancies."

"Long-term use of (acetaminophen) increased the risk of behavior problems by 70 percent at age three. That is considerable."

B. Reference from CNN Health: "Acetaminophen in pregnancy linked to "ADHD-like behaviors" February 24, 2014

http://thechart.blogs.cnn.com/2014/02/24/acetaminophen-in-pregnancy-linked-to-adhd-like-behaviors/

"The data suggests that taking acetaminophen for longer periods and later in pregnancy is associated with higher risks, Ritz says. When women reported use for 20 weeks or more, their children had a 50% increased risk for receiving ADHD medication, according to the study."

67. "When comparing the vitamin content most foods have had a drop of 75% in vitamin A and 50% in vitamin C."

Reference from Healthy You Naturally: "Do Fruits and Veggies Have Enough Nutrients Today"

https://www.healthyyounaturally.com/edu/enough_nutrients.htm

"In the USA, UK and Canada the results were almost identical. The U.K. research was published in the British Food Journal, a peer-reviewed, scientific publication and according to the reports data on nutritional comparisons:

80% of foods tested showed a substantial drop in Calcium and Iron

75% had a large drop in Vitamin A

50% lost considerable Vitamin C and Riboflavin

33% lost thiamine and 12% lost niacin"

"In the analysis, the biggest loser was broccoli, a food that epitomizes healthy eating. All seven of its measurable nutrients showed a massive drop, notably calcium which fell 63% and iron which dropped 34%. It's often cited as a big source of calcium and iron."

"Other examples indicate the amount of vitamin C in sweet peppers has decreased 24% and vitamin A in apples has dropped by 41% according to USDA 1961 vs. 2001 data."

68. "One published study concluded that non-GMO corn compared to GMO corn is twenty times richer in nutrition."

Reference from Prevent Disease: Comparing Vitamin, Mineral, and Energy Content of GMO vs. Non-GMO. Marco Torres, April 16, 2013

69. "Iodine deficiency is also linked to oxidative stress."

A. Reference from World Health Organization: "Iodine deficiency disorders"

http://www.who.int/nutrition/topics/idd/en/

"Iodine deficiency disorders (IDD), which can start before birth, jeopardize children's mental health and often their very survival. Serious iodine deficiency during pregnancy can result in stillbirth, spontaneous abortion, and congenital abnormalities such as ...an irreversible form of mental retardation that affects people living in iodine-deficient areas of Africa and Asia. However, of far greater significance is IDD's less visible, yet pervasive, mental impairment that reduces intellectual capacity at home, in school and at work."

70. "According to the U.S. National Research Council "several lines of information indicate an effect of fluoride exposure on thyroid function."

Reference from Fluoride Alert: "Fifty Reasons To Oppose Fluoridation"

http://fluoridealert.org/articles/50-reasons/

Chapter Five: Does ADHD Ever Go Away?

1. "When the Wall Street Journal asks the question "Why so many babies" a better question would be "Why so few marriages?"

Reference from The Atlantic: The Decline of Marriage and the Rise of Unwed Mothers: An Economic Mystery by Derek Thompson, March 18 2013

"The thesis of this fascinating article in the *Wall Street Journal* says the real mystery here isn't "Why so many babies?" but rather "Why so few marriages?"—particularly among less-educated men and women."

2. "Compared to 1950 there are twice as many single adults."

Reference from The New York Times: Married Couples Are No Longer A Majority, Census finds" by Sabrina Tavernise, May ;26, 2011

http://www.nytimes.com/2011/05/26/us/26marry.html?_r=0

"Married couples represented just 48 percent of American households in 2010, according to data being made public Thursday and analyzed by the Brookings Institution."

"This was slightly less than in 2000, but far below the 78 percent of households occupied by married couples in 1950."

3. "More than two thirds of adult American's are obese or overweight, one out of three are obese, and 17% of children from 2 to 19 are obese"

Reference from US Department of Health and Human Services: "Overweight and Obesity Statistics"

http://win.niddk.nih.gov/publications/PDFs/stat904z.pdf

4. "The number one complaint doctors hear from patients is increased tiredness and fatigue."

Reference from Harvard Health Publications: "Tired of being tired?"

http://www.health.harvard.edu/healthbeat/HEALTHbeat_070308.htm

"Feeling tired all the time? You're not alone. In fact, fatigue is one of the most common complaints that bring adults to doctors' offices. Numerous studies indicate that people who see their doctor about fatigue have generally experienced it for a considerable length of time — anywhere from six months to several years!"

5. "Over thirty million men have erectile dysfunction."

Reference from CNN: Sunday Morning

http://transcripts.cnn.com/TRANSCRIPTS/0308/24/sm.15.html

"About 30 million men have erectile dysfunction, but only one in five seek help."

The down regulation of dopamine receptors in ADHD causes some children to lose interest in an activity unless it is new or novel. In a similar way, for some adults, when their partner is no longer new or novel their interest and attraction goes away. Keep in mind, that ADHD drugs activate dopamine just as having sex with a new partner. Many men report unable to be turned on to their partner but can easily get turned on to Porn or a new relationship.

6. "It is estimated that 1 out of 5 men over forty-five have used these drugs."

Reference from Wall Street Journal: "Viagra is Misunderstood"
http://www.usrf.org/breakingnews/bn_111202_viagra/bn_111202_viagra.html

"More than 20 million men around the world use it regularly. In the U.S., one out of every five men over 40 has tried it. An average of nine Viagra pills are dispensed every second."

"Men and women who use it rarely talk about it openly. But in the U.S., an estimated 34% of all men ages 40 to 70 about 20 million men suffer from some significant level of erectile dysfunction. Most of them, about 80%, never seek treatment."

Chapter Six: How Stimulant Drugs Change Your Child's Brain

1. "Recent brain scans reveal a distinction in brain activity associated with ADHD that can last a lifetime."

Reference From JAMA: "Developmental trajectories of brain volume abnormalities in children and adolescents with attention-deficit/hyperactivity disorder." 2002 Oct 9;288(14):1740-8. Castellanos FX and associates
http://www.ncbi.nlm.nih.gov/pubmed/12365958

"On initial scan, patients with ADHD had significantly smaller brain volumes in all regions, even after adjustment for significant covariates."

"Developmental trajectories for all structures, except caudate, remain roughly parallel for patients and controls during childhood and adolescence, suggesting that genetic and/or early environmental influences on brain development in ADHD are fixed, nonprogressive, and unrelated to stimulant treatment."

2. "One of the main differences between Ritalin and cocaine is that the doses of stimulant drugs for children are smaller than what you would take as a drug addict."

Reference from The Journal of Pharmacology and Experimental Therapeutics: "Blockade of striatal dopamine transporters by intravenous methylphenidate is not sufficient to induce self-reports of "high"". Volkow ND and associates. Jan 1999: 14-20

"Methylphenidate, like other stimulants, increases dopamine levels in the brain, but at therapeutic doses this increase is slow, and thus euphoria only rarely occurs.."

Chapter Seven: The Key To Healing The Brain

1. "Long-term studies have confirmed that on average after using stimulant drugs ADHD symptoms return within three years."

Reference from Dr. Yannick Paul's UnRitalin Solution: "Do ADHD medications work in the long-term?"

http://unritalinsolution.com/adhd_drugs

"MTA study revealed surprising results that contradict what most medical doctors claim. At first, their results showed that children on medications yielded more positive results than children who received only behavioral therapy. This first discovery led to an increase in the use of ADHD medications to treat the disorder. After one year of treatment, the researchers discovered that 48% of children who took ADHD medication showed improvements. They concluded that medications worked. What they did not mention is the fact that 52% of children were still suffering from inattention, hyperactivity, and impulsivity! Not only do traditional medications fail to help half of the children to recover from ADHD; the study also discovered that the efficacy of medications diminishes over time."

"In 2007, the final results of the MTA Study were published and its conclusions were even more surprising: in the long run (after 3 years) there is no evidence to prove that ADHD medications are more effective than taking no medication at all. In fact, ADHD medications actually do more damage than good!"

2. "...the risks of common side effects like stunted growth, weight loss and long-term brain changes must also be considered."

Reference from The New York Times: "Ritalin Gone Wrong" by L. Alan Sroufe, Jan 28,2012

http://www.nytimes.com/2012/01/29/opinion/sunday/childrens-add-drugs-dont-work-long-term.html?pagewanted=all&_r=0

"But when given to children over long periods of time, they neither improve school achievement nor reduce behavior problems. The drugs can also have serious side effects, including stunting growth."

"Many parents who take their children off the drugs find that behavior worsens, which most likely confirms their belief that the drugs work. But the behavior worsens because the children's bodies have become adapted to the drug. Adults may have similar reactions if they suddenly cut back on coffee, or stop smoking."

"To date, no study has found any long-term benefit of attention-deficit medication on academic performance, peer relationships or behavior problems, the very things we would most want to improve."

Chapter Eight: The Long-Term Side Effects of Stimulant Drugs

1. "Three times as many boys are diagnoised with ADHD"
Reference from Centers For Disease Control and Prevention: ADHD

http://www.cdc.gov/nchs/fastats/adhd.htm

"Percent of boys 3-17 years of age ever diagnosed with ADHD: 12.0%

Percent of girls 3-17 years of age ever diagnosed with ADHD 4.7%"

2. "….over sixty percent of college graduates are girls and not boys."
A. Reference from CNN Money: "Boys vs. girls: What's behind the college grad gender gap? Ann Fisher March 27, 2013

http://management.fortune.cnn.com/2013/03/27/college-graduation-gender-salaries/

"Not only do women enter college at higher rates than men, but they're less likely to drop out once they get there. Female grads now account for about 60% of U.S. bachelor's degree holders."

3. "Two boys to every girl are suspended or expelled from high school."
Reference from National Center for Education Statistics, Institute of Education Sciences: "Youth Indicators 2011. Chapter 2. School-Related Characteristics. Indicator 14. Suspensions and

Expulsions of High School Students." NCES. U.S. Department of Education, 2011. Web. 19 February 2013. <http://nces.ed.gov/pubs2012/2012026/chap- ter2_14.asp>.

"Differences in rates of suspension were found by sex and race/ethnicity. For instance, in 2007, male high school students had been suspended at a rate that was about twice as high as that of their female peers (32 vs. 17 percent)."

4. "...four times as many males commit suicide."

A. Reference from Psychology Today: Boys to Men by Miles Groth, Ph.D.

http://www.psychologytoday.com/blog/boys-men/201308/young-men-who-commit-suicide

"The suicide rate among college age men is four times greater than among females."

B. Reference from National Institute of Mental Health: Suicide in the U.S.

http://www.nimh.nih.gov/health/publications/suicide-in-the-us-statistics-and-prevention/index.shtml

"Almost four times as many males as females die by suicide"

5. "Pornography has become so addictive and pervasive that globally it is a $98 billion dollar a year industry with 14% in America, 21% in Japan, 27% in south Korea and 29% in China."

Reference from TopTen Reviews: Internet Pornography Statistics By Jerry Ropelato

http://internet-filter-review.toptenreviews.com/internet-pornography-statistics-pg4.html. "Worldwide Pornography Revenues and 2005/2006 U.S. Pornography Revenue Stats Pornography revenues are not necessarily ranked according to population. China topped the list in 2006 with more than $27 billion in pornography revenues. However, South Korea, only the 26th most populous nation on earth according to the

U.S. Census Bureau, is next in line with more than $25 billion in pornography revenues."

6. "Online pornography is so pervasive that 12% of all websites have to do with sex."
Reference from State of Digital: Statistics on Internet Porn
http://www.stateofdigital.com/statistics-on-internet-porn-still-a-major-industry/
"12% of websites on the web are still Porn sites."

7. "The Global sex industry makes billions of dollars every year."
Reference from TopTen Reviews: Internet Pornography Statistics
By Jerry Ropelato
t-filter-review.toptenreviews.com/internet-pornography-statistics-pg2.html

Chapter Nine: Proven Solutions For Increasing Brain Performance

1. "Challenging physical exercise and new movements of the body have proven to create the most dramatic and positive changes in brain development."
Reference from Health Magazine: Brain Games and Exercise
http://www.health.com/health/condition-article/0,,20252861,00.html
"By engaging in activities that require new skills and problem solving, patients can stimulate neuron growth, according to Dr. Gimpel."

2. "At all stages of life, the brain has the potential to regenerate and reorganize itself to compensate for oxidative stress."

Reference from Neurobiology: "Neuroplasticity" June 26, 2010
https://www.stanford.edu/group/hopes/cgi-bin/wordpress/
2010/06/neuroplasticity/

"Even simple brain exercises such as presenting oneself with challenging intellectual environments, interacting in social situations, or getting involved in physical activities will boost the general growth of connections."

3. Dr. Anat Baniel explains, "the moment we pay attention to our movement, the brain resumes growing at a very rapid rate."

Reference from interview with Dr. Anat Baniel and her book *Kids Beyond Limits*. I highly recommend her books as she is doing miracles every day helping children with learning difficulties.

4. "By repeating the hand movements for about two hours over a period of five days significant brain growth occurred."

Reference from Neuroscience: "The musician's brain as a model of neuroplasticity." Thomas f Munte, Eckart Alternmuller and Lutz Jancke, Vol 3 June 2002

http://futureofhealth.s3.amazonaws.com/interviews/transcript/Baniel.pdf

"In musically naïve subjects, training on the piano for two hours per day over five days led to increased excitability of the cortical motor areas...musicians who began their musical training before the age of seven have a larger anterior corpus callosum that controls who started later."

5. "Brain scans of children have revealed that those kids who play musical instruments have significantly more grey matter volume in the brain."

Reference from Parenting Science: "Music and intelligence: A guide for the science-minded" Gwen Dewar 2008-2013

http://www.parentingscience.com/music-and-intelligence.html

"Moreover, brain scans of 9- to 11-year old children have revealed that those kids who play musical instruments have significantly more grey matter volume in both the sensorimotor cortex and the occipital lobes (Schlaug et al 2005)."

6. "In the Urban Dove high school, school administrators collected the lowest performing students from other schools and helped them become high achieving students."

Reference from Urban Dove Charter School: "Full Proposal"

http://www.p12.nysed.gov/psc/documents/Full_App_ Urban_Dove_CS_Sept_2010REDACT.pdf

"To date, 98% of Urban Dove's participants have graduated from high school, with more than 90% going onto college."

7. "Art therapy has shown to help students with ADHD reduce impulsive behaviors, enhance interpersonal behavior and improve study skills and classroom performance."

Reference from International Art Therapy Organization: "Art Therapy In Schools"

http://www.internationalarttherapy.org/SchoolArtTherapy. pdf

"Art making has also been shown to enhance cognitive abilities, improve social skills, and encourage self- esteem in school-age children…. For example, an art therapist working with a child with ADHD may develop activities to help reduce impulsive behaviors, enhance interpersonal behavior, and improve study skills and classroom performance."

8. "For all children using art to increase activity on the right side of the brain has shown to increase grades and improve behavior in children."

Reference from Education Week: Does Studying the Arts Enhance Academic Achievement? Ellen Winner and Lois Hetland

http://www.edweek.org/ew/articles/2000/11/01/09winner.h20.html

"The report justifies this claim by noting that both math and verbal SAT scores are higher for students who take the arts than for those who take no arts courses."

9. "According to Brain Mayne, this process of "Goal Mapping" has assisted over 100,000 children to improve brain performance by activating the whole of their brain through the combined use of words and pictures."

Reference from Lift International: "Goal Mapping For Kids"

http://www.liftinternational.com/goal-mapping/kids.html

"...over 100,000 children have created Goal Maps to improve their lives."

Chapter Ten: Natural Supplements Outperform Prescribed Drugs

1. "The results show a significant reduction of hyperactivity and improved concentration. In the placebo group no positive effects were found."

Reference from European Adolescent Psychiatry: "Treatment of ADHD with French maritime pine bark extract, Pycnogenol."

Trebaticka J, Kopasova S, Hradecna Z, et al. Treatment of ADHD with French maritime pine bark extract, Pycnogenol®. *Eur Child Adolesc Psychiatry.* 2006 May 13.

"Results show that 1-month Pycnogenol administration caused a significant reduction of hyperactivity, improves attention and visual-motoric coordination and concentration of children with ADHD."

2. "The short-term benefits in both groups were the same except the natural supplement group had no side effects."
Reference from Livestrong.com: "OPC-3 Isotonix for ADHD" by Rachel Elizabeth

http://www.livestrong.com/
article/525476-opc-3-isotonix-for-adhd/

"A preliminary study conducted by Dr. Marion Sigurdson, a psychologist, used an OPC supplement made from pine bark and grape seed to treat 30 children and adults with ADHD. She said it worked as well as stimulant medication in treating attention and behavior symptoms."

3. "The results were so miraculous that PBS made a documentary of the success."
Reference from Eat, Exercise and Excel
http://vimeo.com/18776015

4. "In another case study researchers confirmed that a monitored program of amino acid supplementation with over the counter supplements, such as l-tyrosine, 5-htp, l-cysteine and a multivitamin could stop the progression of Parkinson's disease without side effects and in many cases even reverse the symptoms."
Reference from International Journal of General Medicine: "Amino acid management of Parkinson's disease: a case study" by Marty Hinz, Alvin Stein, and Thomas Uncini.

http://www.ncbi.nlm.nih.gov/pmc/articles/PMC3068871/

5. "A modified version of this program was found to completely reverse symptoms of ADHD."

Reference from Neuropsychiatric Disease and Treatment: "Treatment of attention-deficit hyperactivity disorder with monoamine amino acid precursors and organic cation transporter assay interpretation."

http://www.ncbi.nlm.nih.gov/pmc/articles/PMC3035600/

"This analysis does provide some initial evidence of the efficacy of amino acids in significantly reducing symptoms associated with ADHD. Tables 9 and 10 reveal the efficacy of this treatment protocol to be potentially superior to results seen with prescription drugs."

6. "DHA omega three has also been shown to improve learning and memory and support cognitive health with aging"

Reference from Alzheimer's, Dementia: "Beneficial effects of docosahexaenoic acid (DHA) on cognition in age-related cognitive decline." Yurko-Mauro K1, McCarthy D, Rom D, Nelson EB, Ryan AS, Blackwell A, Salem N Jr., Stedman M; MIDAS Investigators. November 2010

"Twenty-four week supplementation with 900 mg/d DHA improved learning and memory function in ARCD and is a beneficial supplement that supports cognitive health with aging."

7. "A study in India demonstrated that supplementation with flax oil (rich in omega 3) and vitamin C provided significant improvement in children with ADHD."

Reference from Science Direct: "Supplementation with flax oil and vitamin C improves the outcome of Attention-deficit Hyperactivity Disorder (ADHD) Kalpana Joshi and associates October 16, 2005

http://www.declareamor.com.br/wp-content/uploads/2012/07/Óleo-de-Linha-e-Vitamina-C..pdf

"There was significant improvement in the symptoms of ADHD reflected by reduction in total hyperactivity scores of ADHD children derived from ADHD rating scale."

8. "An Australian study has shown that the use of omega 3 fish oils is more effective for treating ADHD than Ritalin and Concerta, the drugs most often prescribed for ADHD in Australia."

Reference from Natural News: "Fish oils treat ADHD better than prescription drugs, study shows" June 20, 2006

http://www.naturalnews.com/019432_fish_oil_nutrition.html#ixzz2tc9u5srY

"According to the results of a new study from the University of South Australia, fish oil is more effective at treating children with attention-deficit hyperactivity disorder (ADHD) than stimulant drugs, such as commonly prescribed Ritalin."

9. "To counteract this tendency, one or two grams of acetyl-l-carnitine a day can assist the body in utilizing the omega three supplements."

Reference from ADHD Treatments: "Ten Ways Carnitine can help treat ADHD"

http://adhd-treatment-options.blogspot.com/2009/04/10-ways-carnitine-can-help-treat-adhd.html

"For a one year study on the effects of carnitine for ADHD boys, a daily dose of 1000 mg per day was found to be safe. This study recommended 20-50 mg carnitine per kg of body weight, which is roughly one fifth to one half of the levels used in the Dutch study." (100 pounds is about 50 kg so at 20 mgs per kg the low dose is 1000mg for a 100 pound child.)

10. "At the end of six months participants taking the supplement experienced a significant improvement in memory."

Clinical Intervention Aging: The effect of soybean-derived phosphatidylserine on cognitive performance in elderly with subjective memory complaints: a pilot study, Yael Richter, Yael Herzog, Yael Lifshitz, Rami Hayun, and Sigalit Zchut, 2013

"This exploratory study demonstrates that SB-PS may have favorable effects on cognitive function in elderly with memory complaints."

11. "Study results revealed that participants taking the supplements had a significant improvement in mood and a reduction in AHDA behavior when compared to those given the placebo."

Reference from European Psychiatry: "The effect of phosphatidylserine containing Omega3 fatty acids on attention-deficit hyperactivity disorder symptoms in children: A double-blind placebo-controlled trial, followed by an open-label extension" Manor and associates, July 2012

http://www.sciencedirect.com/science/article/pii/S0924933811000952

"The results of this 30-week study suggest that PS-Omega3 may reduce ADHD symptoms in children. Preliminary analysis suggests that this treatment may be especially effective in a subgroup of hyperactive-impulsive, emotionally and behaviorally-dysregulated ADHD children."

12. "The results showed that PS produced significant improvements in attention, hyperactivity, impulsive behaviors and short-term auditory memory."

Reference from Journal of Human Nutrition and Dietetics: "The effect of phosphatidylserine administration on memory and symptoms of attention-deficit hyperactivity disorder: a randomized, double-blind, placebo-controlled clinical trial" S.Hirayama and associates, 17, March 2013

http://onlinelibrary.wiley.com/doi/10.1111/jhn.12090/abstract

Chapter Eleven: Homeopathy and Body Work Can Heal Concussion

1. "Studies show that children who have a history of concussion are more likely to develop ADHD and have difficulty controlling their moods."

"Furthermore, children who have a history of concussion are more likely to develop attention-deficit hyperactivity disorder (ADHD) and have difficulty controlling their moods, especially anger, rather than experience depression."

2. "Older athletes, who suffered from concussions while playing football, later in life are having symptoms similar to Parkinson's as well as memory loss and ADHD."

Reference from Medical News Today: "Concussions Cause Long-Term Effects Lasting Decades" February, 2013

http://www.medicalnewstoday.com/articles/256518.php

"The results indicate that there is abnormal brain wave activity for years after a concussion, as well partial wasting away of the motor pathways, which can lead to significant attention problems."

"A recent study was carried out comparing healthy athletes to those of the same age who suffered from a concussion 30 years ago. The results showed that those who experienced head trauma had symptoms similar to those of early Parkinson's disease - as well as memory and attention deficits. "

3. "From research at the university of California they found that after a concussion about 10 percent of kids had a full depressive disorder 6 months later."

Reference from Psych Central: "Teen Concussions Raise Risk for Depression" 1/19/2014 http://www.sciencedaily.com/releases/2014/01/140109175502.htm

"In our research, we've found that about 10 percent of the kids had a full depressive disorder or subclinical depressive disorder 6 months after a concussion," said Jeffrey Max, M.D., a psychiatrist who specializes in psychiatric outcomes of traumatic brain injury in children and adolescents at the University of California, San Diego."

4. "It was assumed that "the brain will recover at it's on pace within 7 to 10 days."

Reference from Medicine Net: "Brain Concussion," Benjamin Wedro, MD,

http://www.medicinenet.com/brain_concussion/page4.htm

"Brain rest is an important concept. In today's high tech connected world, the brain is often asked to process information at a high rate of speed from television, computers, and smartphones. Limiting use of those devices may be helpful in allowing the brain to recover more quickly."

"Ultimately, the brain will recover at its own pace. While 80% to 90% of concussion patients will recover within 7 to 10 days, some patients will experience symptoms for weeks or months. The length of recovery is not necessarily related to the initial injury."

5. "One of the best designed double-blind studies for alternative medicine has demonstrated homeopathy's effectiveness in treating concussions."

Reference from Head Trauma Rehabilitation: "Homeopathic treatment of mild traumatic brain injury: A randomized, double-blind, placebo-controlled clinical trial." E.H. Chapman and associates, 1999 volume 14, pg. 521-42

http://www.ncbi.nlm.nih.gov/pubmed/10671699

"These results indicate a significant improvement from the homeopathic treatment versus the control and translate into clinically significant outcomes."

"This study suggests that homeopathy may have a role in treating persistent MTBI."

6. "In one study, 90% of soldiers practicing EFT no longer met the criteria for clinical PTSD compared with only 4% of the control group."

Reference from Examiner.com: "Study Shows EFT significantly reduces PTSD in veterans"

http://www.examiner.com/article/study-shows-eft-significantly-reduces-ptsd-veterans-part-1-of-3

"A new randomized controlled study published on Friday, Feb 1, 2013, in the Journal of Nervous and Mental Diseases confirms that Emotional Freedom Techniques (EFT) is an effective treatment for PTSD."

Chapter Twelve: HT Therapy for ADHD and Autism

1. "For example, even today German health insurance gives heart disease patients a choice: they can receive drugs for heart disease or they can take a two-week trip to a German spa for hydrotherapy."

Reference from Wikipedia: Spa

"In Germany, the tradition survives to the present day. 'Taking a cure' (http://de.wikipedia.org/wiki/Kur) at a spa is covered by both public and private health care insurance, as mandated by federal legislation. Typically, a doctor prescribes a few weeks stay at a mineral spring or other natural setting where a patient's condition will be treated with healing spring waters and natural therapies."

2. "Recently, in 2013, one clinical study was done with 40 Autistic children."

Reference from Mail Online: "A hot bath 'helps soothe the symptoms of autism and make children more sociable" Fiona Macrae, Dec 12, 2013

http://www.dailymail.co.uk/health/article-2522714/Autism-symptoms-soothed-hot-bath.html

3. "During a fever, more immune factors are released to heal the brain."

Reference from Yale Journal of Biological Medicine: "Is fever beneficial to the host: a clinical perspective." G.W. Duff, 1986

http://www.ncbi.nlm.nih.gov/pubmed/3488618

"Recent advances in the biology of interleukin-1 and other cytokines have allowed the testing, in vitro, of components of mammalian host defense (such as immune cell function) at temperatures typical of fever, and marked effects have been found."

4. "Mothers of autistic children have reported that during a fever, their children's symptoms of autism have disappeared only to reappear after the fever is over."

Reference from WebMD: Report: "Fever Improves Autism Symptoms,"

Salynn Boyles, Dec. 2007

http://www.webmd.com/brain/autism/news/20071203/report-fever-improves-autism-symptoms

"Anecdotal reports of improvements in autism symptoms related to fever have circulated for years, but the research represents the first scientific investigation into the observed association. While kids with autism might be expected to be calmer and less hyperactive when they have fevers, the improvement in communication and socialization seen in the study suggests that fever directly affects brain function, pediatric neurologist Andrew Zimmerman, MD, of Baltimore's Kennedy Krieger Institute, tells WebMD."

5. "More than 80% of children in one study showed improvement in behavior during temperature elevations."

Reference from WebMD: Report: "Fever Improves Autism Symptoms,"

Salynn Boyles, Dec. 2007

http://www.webmd.com/brain/autism/news/20071203/report-fever-improves-autism-symptoms

"More than 80% of the children with fever in the study showed some improvement in behavior during temperature elevations, the researchers reported in the December issue of the journal *Pediatrics*."

"One theory is that fever may affect brain function at the cellular level by influencing the production of immune system signaling proteins known as cytokines."

"If this proves to be the case, the finding could result in treatments for autism spectrum disorders that target cytokine expression.

Chapter Thirteen: Elimination Diets Reverse ADHD

1. "The FDA lists 33 double-blind clinical trials demonstrating that artificial food colors are related to ADHD and other childhood related problem behaviors."

Reference from FDA: "Reviews And Critiques, 33 Clinical Trials Related To Artificial Food Colors And ADHD In Childhood And Related Problem Behaviors, Thomas J. Sobotka, Ph.D., Aug 23, 2010

http://www.fda.gov/downloads/AdvisoryCommittees/CommitteesMeetingMaterials/FoodAdvisoryCommittee/UCM248124.pdf

2. "Food allergies and indigestion trigger inflammation in the brain, which results in different degrees of ADHD."

A. Reference from ABC News: ADHD From Allergy? Study Shows Benefit From Diet Changes by Courtney Hutchison via Good Morning America

http://abcnews.go.com/Health/Allergies/adhd-food-allergy-case-restricting-diet/story?id=12832958

"In kids with ADHD, researchers found that putting them on a restrictive diet to eliminate possible, previously unknown food allergies or sensitivities decreased hyperactivity for 64 percent of kids."

B. Reference from US News: Allergies, Asthma Show Links to ADHD: Study" by Serena Gordon, Aug 23, 2013

http://health.usnews.com/health-news/news/articles/2013/08/23/allergies-asthma-show-links-to-adhd-study

"Of those in the study, boys newly diagnosed with ADHD were 40 percent more likely to have asthma, 50 percent more likely to have needed a prescription for allergy medicine and 50 percent more likely to have had a bacterial skin infection than other boys."

"They also found weaker associations between ADHD and cow's milk intolerance, and prescriptions for oral or topical corticosteroids, antibacterial or antifungal drugs."

3. "The most well-known elimination diet proven to reverse ADHD 50% of the time is the Feingold elimination diet."

Reference from http://www.feingold.org/Research/PDFstudies/list.html

4. "By eliminating these foods, along with processed foods containing artificial food colorings and additives, for the majority of children, the symptoms of ADHD, quickly go away."

Reference from Diagnosis - Diet: "Food Sensitivities and ADHD" By Georgia Ede MD

http://diagnosisdiet.com/food-sensitivities-and-adhd/

This is a great site as Dr. Ede lists a variety of simplified diets that have helped and sometimes cured ADHD.

5. "Almost 90 percent of children with ADHD have some degree of chronic colitis."

A. Reference from the American Journal of Gastroenterology: "Enterocolitis in children with developmental disorders" A.J. Wakefield and associates, 2000.

http://www.nature.com/ajg/journal/v95/n9/abs/ajg 2000579a.html

This study was very controversial and eventually redacted but below in reference B are 11 peer-reviewed studies supporting the original findings of Wakefield and colleagues at the Royal Free Hospital in the UK.

B. Reference from Homeopathy Center Of Houston: "Age of Autism"

http://www.ageofautism.com/2010/05/peer-reviewed-papers-support-findings.html

6. "Using this program Dr. Cambell-McBride cured her three-year-old son's autism."

Reference from http://www.gapsdiet.com

Order Book Two
Staying Focused In A Hyper World
Decreasing Stress To Increase Happiness, Passion And Vitality

marsvenus.com/book-two

Order Book Three
Staying Focused
In A Hyper World
Super Fuel To Relax And
Recharge Your Brainpower

marsvenus.com/book-three

We look forward
to hearing
your experiences
and feedback!

Email Us:
share@marsvenus.com

Made in the USA
Middletown, DE
12 July 2015